ASHE Higher Education Report: Volume 43, Number 2
Kelly Ward, Lisa E. Wolf-Wendel, Series Editors

AF278444

Faculty Members' Scholarly Learning Across Institutional Types

Vicki L. Baker, Aimee LaPointe Terosky,

Edna Martinez

Faculty Members' Scholarly Learning Across Institutional Types
Vicki L. Baker, Aimee LaPointe Terosky, Edna Martinez
ASHE Higher Education Report: Volume 43, Number 2
Series Editors: Kelly Ward, Lisa E. Wolf-Wendel

ASHE HIGHER EDUCATION REPORT, (Print ISSN: 1551-6970; Online ISSN: 1554-6306), is published quarterly by Wiley Subscription Services, Inc., a Wiley Company, 111 River St., Hoboken, NJ 07030-5774 USA.
Postmaster: Send all address changes to *ASHE HIGHER EDUCATION REPORT*, John Wiley & Sons Inc., C/O The Sheridan Press, PO Box 465, Hanover, PA 17331 USA.

Information for subscribers
ASHE HIGHER EDUCATION REPORT is published in 6 issues per year. Institutional subscription prices for 2017 are:
Print & Online: US$477 (US), US$557 (Canada & Mexico), US$626 (Rest of World), €406 (Europe), £323 (UK). Prices are exclusive of tax. Asia-Pacific GST, Canadian GST/HST and European VAT will be applied at the appropriate rates. For more information on current tax rates, please go to www.wileyonlinelibrary.com/tax-vat. The price includes online access to the current and all online back-files to January 1st 2013, where available. For other pricing options, including access information and terms and conditions, please visit www.wileyonlinelibrary.com/access.

Delivery Terms and Legal Title
Where the subscription price includes print issues and delivery is to the recipient's address, delivery terms are **Delivered at Place (DAP)**; the recipient is responsible for paying any import duty or taxes. Title to all issues transfers FOB our shipping point, freight prepaid. We will endeavor to fulfill claims for missing or damaged copies within six months of publication, within our reasonable discretion and subject to availability.

Back issues: Single issues from current and recent volumes are available at the current single issue price from cs-journals@wiley.com.

Disclaimer
The Publisher and Editors cannot be held responsible for errors or any consequences arising from the use of information contained in this journal; the views and opinions expressed do not necessarily reflect those of the Publisher and Editors, neither does the publication of advertisements constitute any endorsement by the Publisher and Editors of the products advertised.

Publisher: ASHE HIGHER EDUCATION REPORT is published by Wiley Periodicals, Inc., 350 Main St., Malden, MA 02148-5020.

Journal Customer Services: For ordering information, claims and any enquiry concerning your journal subscription please go to www.wileycustomerhelp.com/ask or contact your nearest office.
Americas: Email: cs-journals@wiley.com; Tel: +1 781 388 8598 or +1 800 835 6770 (toll free in the USA & Canada).
Europe, Middle East and Africa: Email: cs-journals@wiley.com; Tel: +44 (0) 1865 778315.
Asia Pacific: Email: cs-journals@wiley.com; Tel: +65 6511 8000.
Japan: For Japanese speaking support, Email: cs-japan@wiley.com.
Visit our Online Customer Help available in 7 languages at www.wileycustomerhelp.com/ask

Production Editor: Abha Mehta (email: abmehta@wiley.com).

Wiley's Corporate Citizenship initiative seeks to address the environmental, social, economic, and ethical challenges faced in our business and which are important to our diverse stakeholder groups. Since launching the initiative, we have focused on sharing our content with those in need, enhancing community philanthropy, reducing our carbon impact, creating global guidelines and best practices for paper use, establishing a vendor code of ethics, and engaging our colleagues and other stakeholders in our efforts. Follow our progress at www.wiley.com/go/citizenship

View this journal online at wileyonlinelibrary.com/journal/aehe

Wiley is a founding member of the UN-backed HINARI, AGORA, and OARE initiatives. They are now collectively known as Research4Life, making online scientific content available free or at nominal cost to researchers in developing countries. Please visit Wiley's Content Access - Corporate Citizenship site: http://www.wiley.com/WileyCDA/Section/id-390082.html

Printed in the USA by The Sheridan Group.

Address for Editorial Correspondence: Coeditors-in -chief, Kelly Ward, Lisa E. Wolf-Wendel, ASHE HIGHER EDUCATION REPORT, Email: lwolf@ku.edu and kaward@wsu.edu

Abstracting and Indexing Services
The Journal is indexed by Academic Search Alumni Edition (EBSCO Publishing); Education Index/Abstracts (EBSCO Publishing); ERIC: Educational Resources Information Center (CSC); Higher Education Abstracts (Claremont Graduate University); IBR & IBZ: International Bibliographies of Periodical Literature (KG Saur).

Cover design: Wiley
Cover Images: ©

For submission instructions, subscription and all other information visit:
wileyonlinelibrary.com/journal/aehe

Advisory Board

The ASHE Higher Education Report Series is sponsored by the Association for the Study of Higher Education (ASHE), which provides an editorial advisory board of ASHE members.

Contents

Executive Summary   **9**

Acknowledgements   **12**

Foreword   **13**

Introduction   **16**

Challenges to Faculty Scholarly Learning   17

Opportunities to Support Faculty Scholarly Learning   18

Advancing Scholarly Learning Across Institution Types   20

Monograph Purpose and Guiding Questions   20

Monograph Overview   22

Conceptualizing Scholarly Learning and Boyer's Forms
of Scholarship   **23**

Defining Learning   23

Defining Scholarly Learning   24

Significance of Scholarly Learning in the Academic Career   26

Defining Boyer's Forms of Scholarship   27

Conclusion: Connecting Scholarly Learning, Boyer, and
Institutional Type   30

Research Universities   **31**

Defining Research Universities and Their Students and Faculty   31

Mission   31

Students   32

Faculty   33

Challenges   35
Summary   37
Faculty Scholarly Learning in Research Universities   37
  Scholarship of Discovery   38
  Scholarship of Teaching   40
  Scholarship of Engagement   42
  Scholarship of Integration   45
Barriers to Scholarly Learning in Research Universities   46
  Valued Versus Rewarded   47
  Increased Demands for Competition and Productivity   47
  Academic Capitalism   48
Opportunities for Scholarly Learning in Research Universities   49
  Scholarly Learning Through High-Impact Practices   49
  Increasing Opportunities for Collaboration with Internal and
    External Stakeholder   50
  Institutional Service to Support Scholarly Learning   50
Conclusion and Implications   51

Comprehensive Colleges and Universities   **53**
Defining Comprehensives and Their Students and Faculty   53
  Mission   54
  Students   55
  Faculty   55
  Challenges   56
Faculty Scholarly Learning at Comprehensives   57
  Scholarship of Discovery   59
  Scholarship of Teaching   60
  Scholarship of Engagement   62
  Scholarship of Integration   63
  Summary of Faculty Scholarly Learning in Comprehensives   63
Barriers to Faculty Scholarly Learning at Comprehensives   64
  Workload Challenges   64
  Mission Confusion   65

Lack of Resources   66
Opportunities for Faculty Scholarly Learning at Comprehensives   66
   Broadening Views of Scholarship for Comprehensive Faculty   66
   Developing an Infrastructure of Support   67
Conclusion and Implications   68

Liberal Arts Colleges   **70**
Defining Liberal Arts Colleges and Their Students and Faculty   70
   Mission   70
   Students   72
   Faculty   72
   Challenges   75
   Summary   76
Faculty Scholarly Learning in Liberal Arts Colleges   76
   Scholarship of Discovery   77
   Scholarship of Teaching   77
   Scholarship of Engagement   80
   Scholarship of Integration   80
Barriers to Faculty Scholarly Learning in Liberal Arts Colleges   81
   Inaccurate Assumptions About Academic Work in LACs   82
   Inadequate Faculty Development Supports   83
   Disconnect Between Expectations and Reward/Incentive
     Structures   83
Opportunities for Scholarly Learning in Liberal Arts Colleges   84
   Redefining Faculty Learning in LACs   84
   Modernizing Faculty Development Supports   85
   Aligning Policy and Practice   85
Conclusions and Implications   86

Community Colleges   **88**
Defining Community Colleges and Their Students and Faculty   88
   Mission   89
   Students   90
   Faculty   90

Challenges   93
Summary   94
Faculty Scholarly Learning at Community Colleges   94
   Scholarship of Discovery   95
   Scholarship of Teaching   96
   Scholarship of Engagement   98
   Scholarship of Integration   99
   Summary of Faculty Scholarly Learning in Community
      Colleges   100
Barriers to Faculty Scholarly Learning at Community Colleges   100
   Heavy Teaching Loads   101
   Narrow Views of Scholarship   101
   Limited Resources and Infrastructures   102
Opportunities for Faculty Scholarly Learning at Community
   Colleges   103
   Reducing Teaching Loads   103
   Expanding View of Scholarship   103
   Enhancing Resources and Infrastructures   104
Conclusion and Implications   105

A Call to Action: Advancing the Study of Faculty Scholarly
Learning   **107**
Synthesis of Key Findings and Implications   107
Barriers to Scholarly Learning Across All Institution Types:
   Implications for Research   111
   Narrow Views of Academic Work and Scholarship   112
   Contradictory and Unclear Faculty Evaluation and Reward
      Systems   113
   Limited Organizational Support and Infrastructures   113
   Workload Issues   114
Opportunities to Support Faculty Scholarly Learning Across All
   Institution Types: Implications for Practice   115
   Broadening or Expanding View of Scholarship   116

Revisiting Workload and Reward Structures   117
    Improving Resources and Infrastructure   117
Future Directions for Research and Scholarship   118
Concluding Thoughts   119

References   **121**

Name Index   **139**

Subject Index   **145**

About the Authors   **148**

Executive Summary

I N A RELATIVELY short period of time, the professoriate has experienced dramatic changes including the erosion of tenure (Nelson, 2010), a rising contingent workforce (Kezar & Maxey, 2012), threats to academic freedom (Reichman, 2015), and a push for faculty members to manage academic work in a more entrepreneurial way (Givens, 2011). As researchers and practitioners of higher education analyze and address the implications of these changes for higher education and its faculty and students, a significant component of the professorial career often gets overlooked—that of faculty members' scholarly learning. Conceptualized by Anna Neumann (2009a), *scholarly learning*, briefly defined as a faculty member's deep engagement in and commitment to a subject matter, is considered the very reason that draws most faculty members into academia. Yet, scholarly learning has been and continues to be largely understudied and misunderstood; oftentimes scholarly learning is only studied in the context of research universities (Neumann, 2009a), thereby failing to acknowledge the ways in which faculty scholarly learning is enacted and supported across institutional types.

In this monograph, we studied more than 400 books, book chapters, peer-reviewed articles, and empirical research studies written about scholarly learning or related content between 2000 and 2016, with an emphasis on four institutional types: research universities, comprehensives, liberal arts, and community colleges; thereby broadening the discussion of scholarly learning beyond the one context of the research university. In order to frame our literature review of scholarly learning at these four institutional types, we employed the work of Ernest Boyer's (1990) *Scholarship Reconsidered* and situated the

---

available literature on faculty learning in his four forms of scholarship: discovery, teaching, engagement, and integration.

The following questions guided this monograph:

- What does scholarly learning, as conceptualized by Neumann (2009a), look like at different types of institutions?
- What contexts and/or supports hinder or help faculty members' scholarly learning at the different institutional types?
- What challenges are noted in the extant literature on faculty work around further study or better understanding of faculty members' scholarly learning across institutional types?

Grounded in these questions, this monograph contributed to the discussion on faculty work by (a) highlighting literature that defines scholarly work and what it looks like across a full range of institution types including research universities, comprehensives, liberal arts, and community colleges; (b) reviewing empirical and practitioner studies that note the best ways to support and advance faculty members' scholarly learning across institution types; (c) expanding the narrative on where scholarly learning takes place beyond the current focus on major research universities and recognizing that scholarly learning occurs in different genres and for different aims (Boyer, 1990); and (d) recognizing the challenges of better understanding scholarly learning at the full range of institution types by highlighting areas for future research and improved practices. This monograph will serve as a resource for current and aspiring higher education researchers, faculty members, professional development practitioners, and academic administrators who are interested in better understanding and supporting the core of academic work—faculty members' scholarly learning.

In the first chapter, we briefly discuss the current state of higher education, particularly in relation to the professoriate. We introduce the notion of scholarly learning and discuss the associated challenges and opportunities. In the second chapter, we define the monograph's conceptual framework of scholarly learning, as viewed through work by Neumann (2009a).

In the third through sixth chapters, we focus on scholarly learning in each of the following institutional types respectively: research universities, comprehensives, liberal arts, and community colleges. To summarize our findings on research universities (third chapter), we note that the scholarship of discovery (i.e., traditional research) is emphasized per the mission of research universities and increasing expectations for research and funding productivity. We also acknowledge that tensions exist around faculty members' time allocations and the valuation of teaching and service at this institutional type, as well as alignment between faculty members' scholarly interests and workload demands. Our findings on comprehensives note that this institutional type is facing confusion around its mission and identity because of continued interest in the scholarship of engagement and teaching, while simultaneously rising expectations around the scholarship of discovery. In regard to liberal arts colleges, this institution's tradition of leading in the scholarship of teaching remains; however, the potential for leadership in other forms of scholarship exists but often remains unknown. To summarize our findings for community colleges, we find that although community college faculty identify as teachers, they also engage in other forms of scholarship.

In sum, an overarching finding of this monograph is as follows: Although mission and academic cultures and norms influence the forms of scholarship engaged in or valued by faculty members across institutional types, our review of the literature highlights that faculty scholarly learning is complex and cannot be described in generic overviews by institutional types. In other words, scholars, policymakers, and practitioners cannot overlook the scholarly interests and passions held by faculty for their own learning and their knowledge expansion and construction (Terosky & Gonzales, 2016), regardless of their employing institutional type. The last chapter discusses if and how the current literature on faculty work expands the notions on where scholarly learning takes place beyond the current focus on major research universities and that scholarly learning occurs in different genres and for different aims (Boyer, 1990) and highlighted areas for future research and improved practices that advance faculty members' scholarly learning across institution types.

Acknowledgments

WE WANT TO thank Lisa Wolf-Wendel and Kelly Ward for the opportunity to write this monograph. We also thank Leslie Gonzales for her support and advice during the writing stage, Ryan Arey and Dáire Ryans for their review and corrections, and Sarah Asklock for her editorial support.

Foreword

BURTON CLARK (1989) in his book, *The Academic Life: Small Worlds, Different Worlds*, was one of the first to write about how the work engaged in by faculty members varies greatly by discipline and by institutional type. Building on the importance of context for how faculty go about their work, in this monograph, *Faculty Members' Scholarly Learning across Institutional Types*, authors Vicki Baker, Aimee LaPointe Terosky, and Edna Martinez revisit and apply Clark's work by looking at the content of what it is that faculty do and also the setting in which they work. The monograph is framed using Neumann's (2009a,b) construct of scholarly learning—a concept that highlights the engagement and commitment to developing faculty expertise—as a way to think about faculty work. Using Ernest Boyer's (1990) broadened definition of scholarship (discovery, teaching, engagement, and integration), the monograph authors make sense of the varied and complicated lives of faculty members within different contexts. The monograph is organized using the scholarly learning construct as expressed through Boyer's views of scholarship and also focused on how faculty work and scholarly learning are manifested in different institutional types. Briefly defined, scholarly learning is faculty engagement in and commitment to their subject matter. It is typically the attraction to developing disciplinary expertise that draws faculty to life as scholars. Regardless of the area of work (i.e., teaching, research, and/or service), faculty members rely on their areas of expertise to contribute to their institutions. Faculty are hired for their disciplinary expertise. A scholarly learning orientation focuses on keeping faculty engaged and committed to the ongoing development of their expertise. Part of retaining the best and brightest in higher education is having robust mechanisms for faculty development, support, and recognition. The significance of scholarly learning is its connection to keeping faculty engaged and generative across career stages and across all areas of work. A scholarly learning framework, as presented by the authors in this monograph, is one that is relevant for institutions to maintain so they can not only recruit but also retain high-quality and diverse faculty. Expertise needs to be nurtured. Too often support for faculty is related to early career; a scholarly learning approach is one that cuts across the career and also in all areas of faculty work. Readers will find information in the monograph that provides a helpful way not only to think about faculty work from a conceptual standpoint but also, more importantly, to look at ways for institutions to support faculty and create environments that recognize and reward learning-oriented perspectives.

The monograph is particularly timely given the neoliberal context of faculty life where there are more faculty working in short-term and nontenure-track appointments and where faculty are increasingly called upon to do more with less. Faculty in all sectors of higher education feel the pressure to be increasingly productive, competitive, and ultimately self-supporting; cumulatively the pressures associated with contemporary faculty life can threaten creativity and the very productivity that is the goal. A cornerstone of faculty life is engagement, learning, and development. In this monograph, the authors detail what faculty work looks like in different settings. Something we really like about the monograph is how useful it can be to help frame conversations that are taking place at institutions across the country that are trying to maintain the values of traditional academic environments (i.e., learning, creativity) at the same time that it is necessary to acknowledge the fiscal realities that require new and creative ways to stay viable. Faculty play a key role in institutional vitality. It behooves institutions to adopt a scholarly learning orientation as a way to support teaching, promote research, and enhance service.

The monograph is sure to be of interest to those who study the academic career, as well as professional development practitioners and academic administrators who are interested in better supporting the needs of their faculty members. Researchers focused on faculty as well as teaching and learning related topics will find the monograph instructive given the broad swath of research that is cited related to faculty work, scholarship, and institutional type. The authors use the literature on topics related to faculty work and scholarly learning that is sure to be a complement to related research topics. Faculty members themselves, along with potential faculty members, will also find this monograph useful as a means of better understanding the kind of work that gets done at different institutional types. The work raises awareness of how scholarly work and learning are framed in different contexts and what is needed to better support those who seek to advance learning.

The monograph is attentive to the nuances associated with faculty work and faculty learning in different institutional types. Too often research about "faculty" is presented absent the distinctions in what faculty do and how teaching, research, and service are shaped by institutional context. The focus in the monograph on institutional types is refreshing, informative, and comprehensive. The use of Boyer's expanded definition of scholarship is also helpful as a way to think about faculty work that is comprehensive. Faculty, administrators, and researchers in different organizational settings will clearly be able to locate their work.

The monograph reads as a companion and update of the O'Meara, La-Pointe Terosky, and Neumann (2008) monograph, *Faculty Careers and Work Lives: A Professional Growth Perspective*. Common across both these pieces is a focus on faculty learning and development—concepts that are more often associated with students. Historically there has been little emphasis on faculty scholarly learning. There also tends to be limited focus on faculty work across institutional types. In higher education, references to learning typically focus on students. Important to keeping a faculty workforce that is holistic and supportive of student learning is a focus on keeping faculty generative by supporting their learning. Given the challenges facing higher education today, it is particularly vital to focus on what faculty do, in what institution context they do it, and how it is that faculty stay vital and learning oriented. The future of higher education depends on it.

Kelly Ward
Lisa Wolf-Wendel

Introduction

I N A RELATIVELY short period of time, the professoriate has experienced dramatic changes including the erosion of tenure (Nelson, 2010), a rising contingent workforce (Kezar & Maxey, 2012), threats to academic freedom (Reichman, 2015), and a push for faculty members to manage academic work in a more entrepreneurial way (Givens, 2011). As researchers and practitioners of higher education analyze and address the implications of these changes for higher education and its faculty and students, a significant component of the professorial career oftentimes gets overlooked—that of faculty members' scholarly learning. Scholarly learning, briefly defined as faculty members' deep engagement in and commitment to a subject matter, is considered the very reason that draws most faculty members into academia, and yet, it has been and continues to be largely understudied and misunderstood (Neumann, 2009b). Despite learning being considered as fundamental to the faculty and student experience, the majority of research about learning focuses on how, and in what ways, students learn (Brown, Bull, & Pendlebury, 2013; Entwistle & Ramsden, 2015). The limited research on faculty scholarly learning is, by and large, situated in the research university setting (Neumann, 2009a), thereby failing to acknowledge the ways in which faculty scholarly learning is enacted and supported across institutional types (an exception includes Terosky and Gonzales, 2016).

With this in mind, we focus on literature about and related to faculty scholarly learning from 2000 to present day, with an emphasis on four institutional types: research universities, comprehensives, liberal arts, and community colleges; thereby broadening the discussion of scholarly learning beyond the one context of the research university. This monograph is grounded in the work of Anna Neumann (2009a,b), in which she puts forth the concept of scholarly learning and the passion it evokes. Moreover, this monograph builds on a previous *ASHE Higher Education* monograph by O'Meara, Terosky, and Neumann (2008), in which they examined faculty professional growth and developed a four-part model that included learning as one part of their model. In order to frame the literature review of scholarly learning at four institutional types, we employ the work of Ernest Boyer's (1990) *Scholarship Reconsidered* and we review the available literature on faculty learning through his four forms of scholarship: discovery, teaching, engagement, and integration (see the second chapter for further discussion of Boyer's forms of scholarship). We argue that such an examination and review of the literature about and related to faculty scholarly learning at a range of institutional types is not only worthy of study but also essential for a full understanding of what drives faculty work across the higher education system during a time of great change.

Challenges to Faculty Scholarly Learning

Critical macro-level (e.g., governmental level, institutional level) and micro-level (e.g., individual faculty member actions) challenges create obstacles to understanding and supporting faculty members' scholarly learning across institution types. Macro-level influences, such as rising accountability and efficiency demands by the public, have shifted research agendas, sought to prescribe how faculty members use their time, and contributed to the workload (and overload) of faculty members. Decreased funding at state and federal levels has resulted in increased reliance on part-time, contingent faculty across institution types (Kezar, 2012), thus increasing competition for traditional full-time tenure-track positions (Huber, 2002) and growing concerns about contingent faculty members' effect on student learning outcomes and classroom learning (Jaeger, 2008). Further, faculty evaluation systems have become more about promotion and tenure processes rather than being used as developmental opportunities (Arreola, 2000; Wright, 2006). At the micro level, changing student demographics and related demands for pedagogical and instructional changes have altered the ways in which teaching and learning are enacted and rewarded (Brint, 2011). Moreover, shifting missions and activities of institutions striving to emulate highly ranked institutions have affected the ways in which faculty engage in academic work (Boyer, Moser, Ream, & Braxton, 2015; Ehrenberg & Zhang, 2005). Faculty members are also tasked with managing an increase in administrative and service requirements because of reduced full-time faculty positions; they must adapt to pedagogical and technological advances and face pressure to publish or obtain funding during competitive economic times (Henderson, 2011; Johnson, 2012; Kezar & Maxey, 2012).

Opportunities to Support Faculty Scholarly Learning

Despite the obstacles noted, institutions of all types are exploring opportunities at the institutional, government, and societal levels to manage these challenges. The work of Cariaga-Lo, Dawkins, Enger, Schotter, and Spence (2010) identified common goals among their group of research participants, one of which is the desire of all campus leaders and administrators to attract, retain, and develop a talented, diverse faculty body. Such goals call for innovation and evoke creativity by way of faculty development initiatives for tenured and tenure-track faculty, as well as contingent and part-time faculty members. For example, Cariaga-Lo and colleagues (2010) cited programs and initiatives such as Harvard's New Faculty Institute (a 2-day conference designed to welcome new faculty members to Harvard) and at Spelman College, a historically Black liberal arts college, faculty meetings to facilitate the pursuit of collaborative course development.

As institutions seek to address challenges to scholarly learning, so too do scholars and practitioners who strive to advance understanding and practice in the fields of faculty development and academic work (Schuster & Finkelstein, 2006; Sorcinelli, Austin, Eddy, & Beach, 2006). In their book, *Faculty Priorities Reconsidered*, O'Meara and Rice (2005) highlighted a concern dating back to the 1980s about the misaligned priorities of faculty and academic work in relation to the central missions of the institutions in which they worked. Other researchers have noted, "Many institutions have not seriously considered how support for faculty must evolve to better enable them to accomplish their work" (Gappa, Austin, & Trice, 2007, p. 4). Sorcinelli (2007) and colleagues (Sorcinelli et al., 2006) conducted a large-scale study of faculty developers to better understand the current state of the faculty development field. Their research revealed, across institution types, the expansion of faculty roles as one of the most important issues facing faculty members on their campuses. This expansion resulted in an intensification of tasks expected of faculty and pressure to keep up with changing teaching and research directions, find ways to support a more diversified student body, and uphold increased research productivity. A changing professoriate requires faculty development programming and related resources to help faculty members navigate these institutional and professional realities.

The extant literature on faculty development pulls from multiple perspectives, including those of campus leaders, administrators, faculty developers, and faculty members (Baker, Lunsford, & Pifer, in press; Beach, Sorcinelli, Austin, & Rivard, 2016; Sorcinelli, Austin, Eddy, & Beach, 2006). This literature has offered (a) guidance and practical approaches to improving faculty development efforts (Baker et al., in press; Robison, 2013; Schroeder, 2012), (b) insights into the perspectives of and factors that influence faculty members' satisfaction and motivation (Baker et al., in press; Blackburn & Lawrence, 1995; Trower, 2012), and (c) direct advice and guidance to the faculty members themselves as a means of providing a realistic job preview of the faculty career (Baker et al., in press; Buller, 2009). Edited volumes featuring faculty development topics have contributed to the study of the professoriate including those by the Professional and Organizational Development Network in Higher Education, including *A Guide to Faculty Development* (Gillespie & Robertson, 2010) and the *To Improve the Academy* series, both of which aim to support higher education, the faculty development field, and the career development of those employed in this sector. The work of Kezar and Sam (2010), *Non-Tenure Track Faculty in Higher Education: Theories and Tensions*, and Kezar and Maxey (2016), *Envisioning the Faculty for the Twenty-First Century: Moving to a Mission-Oriented and Learner-Centered Model*, explores the rising reliance on a contingent faculty workforce and the implications of such faculty appointments on how colleges and universities manage faculty development, hiring, scheduling, and evaluation.

The work of these scholars and practitioners has contributed to the growing conversation about the professoriate, changes to academic work and expectations, and the ways in which administrators, campus leaders, and faculty developers seek to support faculty members as they engage in their evolving roles and responsibilities. However, additional resources are needed to examine these issues more deeply in order to return to the fundamental goal of higher education—a richer understanding of how to foster, support, evaluate, and reward faculty scholarly learning across all areas of academic work *and* institution types.

Advancing Scholarly Learning Across Institution Types

We agree with Burton Clark (1997) when he noted, "We deceive ourselves every time we speak of the college professor, a common habit among popular critics of the professoriate who fail to talk to academics in their varied locations and to listen to what they say" (p. 22). This observation rings true today given faculty work in research universities has informed the majority of what we do know about scholarly learning and academic work, to date. Very little is known about scholarly learning and the various ways in which scholarly learning is facilitated in other institutional settings (exceptions include Henderson, 2011; Terosky & Gonzales, 2016). The literature, summary findings, and implications for research and practice offered in this monograph can serve as a foundation for future research and practice in the area of faculty scholarly learning.

Monograph Purpose and Guiding Questions

The present monograph extends the work of O'Meara et al. (2008) by providing an updated, comprehensive review of research and practice that explores faculty scholarly learning through Boyer's forms of scholarship. O'Meara et al. (2008) reviewed more than 1,000 resources and touched on the four concepts comprising their professional growth model—learning, commitments, professional relationships, and agency. Building on their work, we studied more than 400 books, book chapters, peer-reviewed articles, and empirical research studies written about scholarly learning or related content between 2000 and 2016. With faculty members' scholarly learning being understudied and often misunderstood across the range of institution types in U.S. higher education, this monograph contributes to the conversation on faculty work by (a) highlighting literature that defines scholarly work and what it looks like across a full range of institution types including research universities, comprehensive universities, liberal arts colleges (LACs), community colleges, and minority-serving institutions (MSIs); (b) reviewing empirical and practical studies that note the best ways to support and advance faculty members' scholarly learning across institution types; (c) expanding the narrative on where scholarly learning takes place beyond the current focus on major research universities and acknowledging that scholarly learning occurs in different genres and for different aims (Boyer, 1990); and (d) recognizing the challenges of better understanding scholarly learning at the full range of institution types by highlighting areas for future research and improved practices. The following questions guide this monograph:

- What does scholarly learning, as conceptualized by Neumann (2009a,b), look like at different institutional types?
- What contexts and/or supports hinder or help faculty members' scholarly learning at the different institutional types?
- What challenges are noted in the extant literature on faculty work around further study or better understanding of faculty members' scholarly learning across institutional types?

In sum, we agree with Rhoades's (2007) assessment that "at their core, colleges and universities are bundles of knowledge shaped and defined by academics" (p. 119), and the core purpose of higher education is knowledge expansion and construction. Thus, our aim is to highlight the current literature on faculty members' scholarly learning across institution types so as to understand the state of scholarly learning in today's college/university settings better, as well as to benefit current and future research and practices on how best to support faculty members' scholarly learning across types of institutions. This monograph will serve as a resource for current and aspiring higher education researchers, faculty members, professional development practitioners, and academic administrators who are interested in better understanding and supporting the core of academic work—faculty members' knowledge expansion and construction (Terosky & Gonzales, 2016). Further, this monograph strives to serve as a resource and to raise awareness of the experiences of faculty at different types of institutions, particularly around their scholarly work and learning, and the support they need to advance that learning.

Monograph Overview

The next chapter explains the monograph's conceptual framework of scholarly learning, as viewed through work by Neumann (2009a,b). The third through sixth chapters examine what scholarly learning looks like across institution types, including research universities (third chapter), comprehensive universities (fourth chapter), LACs (fifth chapter), and community colleges (sixth chapter), and when applicable and available, we discuss MSIs within these institutional types. We structure each chapter around Boyer's (1990) four forms of scholarship (i.e., discovery, integration, teaching, and engagement). The seventh chapter responds to two of the key contributions of the monograph: first, by discussing if and how the current literature on faculty work expands the notions on where scholarly learning takes place beyond the current focus on major research universities and that scholarly learning occurs in different genres and for different aims (Boyer, 1990); and second, by highlighting areas for future research and improved practices that advance faculty members' scholarly learning across institution types.

Conceptualizing Scholarly Learning and Boyer's Forms of Scholarship

BEFORE EXAMINING THE scholarly learning of faculty members employed at various institutional types featured in the third through sixth chapters, this chapter defines learning and scholarly learning per the work of Neumann (2009a,b). A discussion of the significance of scholarly learning to the faculty career, including an examination of both the barriers and opportunities to scholarly learning in academic settings, is incorporated. To conclude, Boyer's four forms of scholarship are addressed because his work serves as an organizing structure.

Defining Learning

Despite its significance and centrality in academic careers, scholarly learning is, in actuality, ill defined, understudied, and misunderstood (Neumann, 2005a, 2009b). In order to define scholarly learning, we must define the concept of learning. To do so, we borrow from Neumann (2005a) who stated: "Learning, as changed cognition, involves the personal and shared construction of knowledge; it involves coming to know something familiar in different ways, or to know something altogether new, from within one's self and often with others" (p. 65). In defining learning, Neumann consistently refers to several interrelated claims about learning, specifically that learning is connected to the subject matter, the learner, and the context, which we describe in the following section.

Throughout her writings, Neumann (2005a, 2009a) emphasized that learning cannot be separated from the *subject matter* that is being learned. "Talk and thought about learning," explained Neumann (2005a), "is vague and insubstantial without taking into account what is being learned" (p. 64). Put simply, the "what"—or the disciplinary knowledge, defined as the substantive content that comprises an academic's field of study—is important to the process of learning (Neumann, 2009a, 2014; see also Hermanowicz, 1998).

In addition to the significance of subject matter in learning, Neumann (2005a) also stresses that "Learning implies a *learner* [italics added] (or learners)" (p. 66). She recognizes that learning, and the process of learning, is influenced by individuals' frames of mind that have been shaped by their past and current experiences and reflections on those experiences. Rather than passively receiving information, individuals construct and reconstruct knowledge to form their own mental models of the world (see Dewey, 1933; Freire, 1970; Piaget, 1975).

A third claim about learning asserted by Neumann (2005a, 2009a) is that *context*, particularly the context of individuals' communities, shapes learning. Neumann (2005a) defined context as "sets of interlinked social, cultural, intellectual, and personal affordances (and patterns or absence thereof) within which a focal learning and developing person, relationship, or other entity is nested" (p. 75). Similarly, Lattuca and Creamer (2005) viewed learning as "the personal and shared construction of knowledge," and they noted that "much of what we learn, we learn from our interactions with others" (p. 4).

Defining Scholarly Learning

Neumann (2009a) defines scholarly learning as faculty members' "engagement with a subject that means a great deal to them or to which they have committed themselves deeply throughout their lives" (p. 2). The key aspect of scholarly learning is that it focuses on the *disciplinary knowledge* of a faculty member's expertise, including knowledge and skills within a subject matter and its related interdisciplinary work (Gonzales & Rincones, 2012; Lattuca,

2001). Scholarly learning contrasts with other forms of learning, such as learning of an instrumental nature in which faculty members acquire knowledge and skills that are related to their careers but are not connected to their subject matter expertise (e.g., how to use a data system for administrative tasks, who on the organizational chart performs what task). In contrast to instrumental learning, Neumann (2009a) characterizes scholarly learning by a passion for a subject matter, which typically draws faculty members into academia in the first place.

Building on Neumann's work, Terosky and Gonzales (2016) distinguished between two applications of scholarly learning, that of expanding one's disciplinary knowledge and that of constructing new knowledge for the advancement of one's discipline, teaching, students, and communities. Through their work, Terosky and Gonzales highlighted that scholarly learning not only occurs in traditional forms of research but also through deepening individuals' substantive understanding of their discipline.

With its emphasis on subject matter learning, Neumann (2009a) points out that scholarly learning could occur across the three key areas of responsibilities in the academic career—teaching, service, and research. Although the research domain of the career might be considered more conducive to scholarly learning (e.g., conducting research in one's area of expertise, developing a literature review), Neumann (2009a) and Neumann and Terosky (2007) noted that scholarly learning can also take place in teaching and service. In their study of 40 recently tenured professors at four major research universities, Neumann and Terosky found that participants discussed three ways their service responsibilities benefited their overall learning, one of which was the learning of substance in an area of study (i.e., scholarly learning). Moreover, Neumann and Terosky's participants favorably ranked their service work when it complemented or advanced their subject matter knowledge and/or provided networks with colleagues who could assist, now or in the future, with their scholarly learning.

In sum, faculty learn in many forms as they go about doing their work. For the purposes of this monograph, scholarly learning emphasizes *the learning that takes place within the realm of a faculty members' subject matter expertise.*

Significance of Scholarly Learning in the Academic Career

With all of the concerns facing higher education, why is scholarly learning worthy of attention? Three reasons are offered. First, scholars argue that although faculty members' scholarly learning is considered central to the work of the professoriate, it remains a "black box" (Neumann, 2009a, p. 2) that is largely understudied and misunderstood by higher education stakeholders and the public at large. Moreover, fairly little is known about the scholarly learning of faculty members employed at institutions that are not characterized as major research universities or well-resourced institutions (Dougherty, 2011; Schuster & Finkelstein, 2006). Despite the centrality of scholarly learning in current and aspiring faculty members' passions, personal and professional commitments, and work trajectories, the field has not fully explored how scholarly learning as a conceptual framework and practice can help scholars and practitioners interested in the professoriate better understand faculty members and their work, motivations, and career satisfaction. Without a more thorough understanding of scholarly learning—the very thing that draws higher education's costliest resource, its faculty, to the career—the field of higher education cannot best support its faculty members.

Second, scholars argue that the academic career should be viewed through the lens of a learning enterprise (Neumann, 2009a) because of higher education's central purpose of teaching students and serving the public. If higher education is characterized as a learning enterprise, then it stands to reason that faculty members' scholarly learning—the crux of a learning enterprise—also demands attention and support, especially if colleges and universities strive to uphold their missions and remain competitive and relevant in contemporary society (Gappa, Austin, & Trice, 2007; Hermanowicz, 1998, 2009; Lattuca, 2001; Neumann, 2009a).

A third reason faculty members' scholarly learning is significant relates to faculty vitality and engagement. Faculty members are drawn to the academic career because of a deeply held passion for a subject matter (Neumann, 2009a; see also Gonzales & Rincones, 2012; Hermanowicz, 1998; Neumann, Terosky, & Schell, 2006), alongside a desire to continuously learn within that subject matter (Gappa et al., 2007; Hermanowicz, 1998; Lindholm, 2003; Neumann, 2009a; Trower, 2012). Several studies have found that when faculty spend more time thinking and working on their subject matter expertise, they report more satisfaction with their careers and institutions as well as greater research productivity (Bozeman & Gaughan, 2011). Thus, higher education cannot afford to overlook the significance of scholarly learning in their faculty recruitment, retention, and advancement initiatives. This is particularly relevant if colleges/universities hope to recruit and retain the best and the brightest, especially those who are marginalized and minoritized.

In Neumann's work, as well as in this monograph, it is emphasized that scholarly learning involves expanding or creating knowledge within a faculty member's disciplinary or subject matter expertise. A key focus in scholarly learning is its emphasis on the learning of subject matter knowledge in individual faculty members' areas of expertise. Next, the work of Boyer (1990), which initiated a movement to expand the definition of scholarship, is discussed by defining and outlining four types of scholarship. Boyer's work helps to organize scholarly learning in this monograph given that we argue that scholarly learning occurs in each of Boyer's forms of scholarship.

Defining Boyer's Forms of Scholarship

Scholarly learning emphasized by focusing on one's subject matter expertise can take on different forms and can occur across the range of faculty responsibilities (i.e., teaching, research, service). In order to discuss these forms, the work of Boyer is applied. In his Carnegie report titled, *Scholarship Reconsidered: Priorities of the Professoriate*, Boyer (1990) asserts that the definition of scholarship should be more inclusive than the predominant focus on traditional research and that academe needs to recognize and reward a wider range of scholarly activities. "What we urgently need today," writes Boyer (1990), "is a more inclusive view of what it means to be a scholar—a recognition that knowledge is acquired through research, through synthesis, through practice, and through teaching" (p. 24). Thus, he proposed four forms of scholarship, which included the scholarships of discovery, integration, teaching, and engagement. *It is important to note that, like scholarly learning, the scholarships of discovery, integration, teaching, and engagement emphasize faculty members' learning and working with their subject matter knowledge.* Boyer's forms of scholarship are defined next.

The scholarship of discovery is the traditional definition of research, in which original and empirical studies advance new knowledge and test theories and models. Boyer explains that the scholarship of discovery is the pursuit of knowledge for its own sake and that it is typically disseminated through scholarly publications and presentations. Some examples of the scholarship of discovery include research projects, peer-reviewed articles, books, book chapters, and creative works (e.g., performances, exhibits).

The scholarship of integration synthesizes knowledge across disciplines, topics within a discipline, or time. The purpose of the scholarship of integration is to make connections between disciplines, integrate knowledge from a variety of resources, identify trends in knowledge across disciplines, and create new meanings to knowledge. To Boyer (1990), the scholarship of integration entails "fitting one's own research and the research of others into larger intellectual patterns" (p. 19). Some examples of the scholarship of integration include literature reviews, presentations of interdisciplinary research at conferences, and meta-analysis of a topic or studies across and within a discipline.

The scholarship of teaching is the systematic study of the teaching and learning process, including the development and improvement of pedagogical and curricular practices. It differs from teaching in that the scholarship of teaching requires a format that will allow public sharing and the opportunity for application and evaluation by others. Examples of the scholarship of teaching include the study and dissemination of innovative teaching practices, presentations or peer-reviewed publications about the study or implementation of teaching practices, projects funded by internal or external grants to support instructional activities, and publication of textbooks or teaching materials.

Initially termed the scholarship of application, the scholarship of engagement applies disciplinary knowledge and skills to address important social and institutional problems. The scholarship of engagement relies on faculty members' disciplinary expertise in collaboration with stakeholders to solve real world problems. Like other forms of scholarship, the scholarship of engagement undergoes peer review and its results can be shared with and/or evaluated by peers. Some examples of the scholarship of engagement include consulting activities in fields or industries that connect to a faculty member's subject matter expertise and supporting or developing community-related activities in a field or industry linked to a faculty member's subject matter expertise, and sharing subject matter expertise in a media setting (e.g., radio, newspaper).

Following Boyer's (1990) report, Glassick, Huber, and Maeroff (1997) published *Scholarship Assessed*, which consists of six standards clarifying what each form of scholarship entailed and how each form might be assessed for quality (Glassick et al., 1997; Shulman & Hutchings, 1998). Since the Glassick et al. (1997) report, other scholars have drawn attention to how each form might be evaluated and documented for faculty reward structures (Braxton, Luckey, & Helland, 2002; O'Meara, 2005b, 2005c, 2006, 2011; O'Meara & Rice, 2005) or how to develop and socialize aspiring faculty members around working within and across Boyer's four forms of scholarship (Austin & McDaniels, 2006). Hundreds of colleges and universities have realigned their tenure guidelines and support structures so as to better support multiple forms of scholarship since Boyer's report in 1990 (Braxton, Luckey, & Helland, 2006; Diamond, 1999; Glassick et al., 1997; O'Meara, 2002; O'Meara & Rice, 2005; Rice & Sorcinelli, 2002).

Although the movement to redefine scholarship has made advancements, scholars do highlight areas of concern. First, scholars question whether the redefining scholarship movement, originating from Boyer's work in 1990, has resulted in real reforms in the working conditions and valuation of faculty careers (O'Meara, 2011; O'Meara & Rice, 2005). Second, the literature connecting Boyer's types of scholarship to particular faculty profiles and/or institution types requires additional study. Past studies have noted that institutional differentiation affected Boyer's four forms of scholarship (Braxton et al., 2002) and a common narrative is that certain institutional types value certain types of scholarship (e.g., research universities value the scholarship of discovery, LACs value the scholarship of teaching). However, critics warn against aligning faculty profiles and institution types to specific forms of scholarship because individual faculty members' passions, engagement, and commitments, regardless of their employing institution or demographics, could be overlooked or oversimplified (see Terosky & Gonzales, 2016). Third, scholars discuss concerns about rising workloads for faculty; two concerns tend to garner attention: concerns about striving institutions (O'Meara, 2007) that emulate research universities by valuing research productivity (i.e., scholarship of discovery) without decreasing other faculty responsibilities (e.g., teaching, service, advising), and concerns that faculty members are expected to engage in a fuller range of scholarly activities, per Boyer's framework, without reducing demands for research productivity and outcomes (Gonzales, 2016).

Conclusion: Connecting Scholarly Learning, Boyer, and Institutional Type

The research and practice presented in this monograph focus on the scholarly learning of faculty members employed at various institution types (i.e., research universities, comprehensives, liberal arts, and community colleges), with a particular focus on recent literature (2000 to present) that examines the learning of faculty members that entails their subject matter expertise and knowledge. We organize the literature on faculty members' scholarly learning through Boyer's lens of four types of scholarship (i.e., discovery, integration, engagement, teaching). The next chapter focuses on scholarly learning in research universities.

Research Universities

IN THIS CHAPTER, the scholarly learning of faculty members employed at research universities is examined. The following sections include (a) defining the research university, including key contextual descriptors about their missions, students, and faculty members, (b) examining the work experiences of faculty members, particularly in relation to their scholarly learning per Boyer's framework, and (c) discussing barriers and opportunities to support faculty scholarly learning in research universities.

Defining Research Universities and Their Students and Faculty

Mission

When Johns Hopkins University opened its doors in 1876, the U.S. research university was born. Although rooted in the distinctive history of the prestigious private colleges of the colonial era (Graham & Diamond, 1997), the research university model of education combines undergraduate instruction from the English colleges, the research emphasis from 19th-century German universities, and "the homegrown concept of service to society" (Altbach, Gumport, & Johnstone, 2001, p. 2). Despite educating undergraduate students and supporting this vital mission, the primary goal of the research university is the production and dissemination of new knowledge, and it is this goal, not the fulfillment of an undergraduate teaching mission, that has made U.S. universities the best in the world (Altbach & Salmi, 2011; Cole, 2016).

A research university is defined as a public or private 4-year institution that offers a range of undergraduate, master's, and doctoral degree programs.

Of the doctoral degree programs, at least 20 research/scholarship doctoral degrees are awarded. Research universities' primary mission is to engage in research, with a national focus, as determined by the level of research activity and per-capita research activity.

Today, the 2015 Carnegie Classification categorizes research universities in one of three ways: Doctoral Universities Highest (R1), Higher (R2), and Moderate Research Activity (R3). Inclusion criteria have also changed most notably related to the number of doctoral degrees awarded (e.g., includes institutions that award at least 20 research/scholarship doctoral degrees), noting that this excludes professional practice doctoral-level degrees such as the JD and MD, for example, as well as special focus institutions and tribal colleges. Additionally, institutions were placed in one of three categories according to research and development expenditures. Currently, 115 institutions are classified as R1, 107 as R2, and 113 as R3 (Carnegie Classification of Institutions of Higher Education, 2016).

Students

According to the Carnegie Classification of Institutions of Higher Education (2016), the 115 R1 research universities enroll 3,323,616 students, representing 16.2% of total undergraduate enrollment in the United States. Average enrollment per institution in this category is 28,901 students. The 107 institutions categorized as R2 enroll 1,691,059 students representing 8.3% of total undergraduate enrollment in the United States. Average enrollment for this institution type is 15,804. Finally, the 113 R3 universities enroll 1,464,093 students representing 7.1% of total undergraduate enrollment in the United States. Average enrollment for this institution type is 12,957 students.

The race/ethnicity of students enrolled in public research universities was 2,612,923 (72%) White, 355,490 (10%) Black, 294,693 (8%) Hispanic, 318,678 (9%) Asian/Pacific Islander, and 32,826 (1%) Native American/Alaska Native (National Center for Education Statistics [NCES], 2008). At private research universities, the totals equate to 692,750 (68%) White, 103,743 (10%) Black, 87,379 (9%) Hispanic, 122,795 (12%) Asian/Pacific Islander, and 5,811 (1%) American Indian/Alaska Native (NCES, 2008). All figures are for U.S. institutions.

Faculty

In 2001, Trow discussed the "decline in the university as a community" (p. 113) because of increasing workloads, increases in contingent workers/decreases in tenure-track positions, and the changing nature of academic work. Schuster and Finkelstein (2006) note that although research and doctoral universities employed nearly 50% of all full-time faculty members in 1969, that percentage dropped to 42.2% by 1998.

Given the mission of research universities, it is likely no surprise that researchers have revealed an increase in research productivity across U.S. research universities over time (Dey, Milem, & Berger, 1997; Indiana University, 2016). Some argue the reasons for this increase in research productivity can be attributed to a continuing trend of decreased funding, thus increasing the need for faculty members to be more entrepreneurial in seeking external support to fund research initiatives (Etzkowitz, 2003). Time allocation studies support the research emphasis while shedding light on the various tasks on which research university faculty members spend their time.

The most recent time allocation study for research university faculty members was conducted by Indiana University's Center for Postsecondary Research in the College of Education through the Faculty Survey of Student Engagement (FSSE). FSSE (Indiana University, 2016) study results supported past findings that research university faculty members spend the greatest amount of time on research, compared to peers employed in other institution types (as discussed in the fourth through sixth chapters). Differences exist between those faculty members who teach lower division courses as compared to upper division courses. Faculty members in lower division courses spent 22.07 hours on teaching, 4.56 hours on advising, 8.82 hours on research, and 8.10 hours on service, whereas faculty members who teach upper division courses spent 20.39 hours on teaching, 5.31 hours on advising, 11.56 hours on research, and 9.36 hours on service. However, as evidenced by Table 1, research university faculty members spent the majority of their time engaged in teaching (including teaching-related activities such as course preparation and grading). Furthermore, research university faculty members, at least according to FSSE data, also spend the greatest amount of time on

TABLE 1
FSSE Time Allocation, Hours per Week, in Research Universities

	Research University Lower Division	Research University Upper Division
Teaching	22.07	20.39
Advising	4.56	5.31
Research	8.82	11.56
Service	8.10	9.36
TOTALS	*43.55*	*46.62*

service in comparison to their faculty peers employed at other institution types (see the fourth through sixth chapters).

Findings from the FSSE data align with prior work conducted by Milem, Berger, and Dey (2000), who examined the relationship between institution type and changes in faculty role performance over time. Relying on three national surveys of college and university faculty members from the American Council on Education (http://www.acenet.edu/) and the Higher Education Research Institute (https://heri.ucla.edu/), their sample included research universities, doctoral universities, comprehensive universities, LACs, and 2-year colleges. Milem et al. (2000) found a general and significant increase in time spent engaged in research at all 4-year institutions with faculty members at research universities reporting the greatest amount of time spent engaged in research. Further, findings also revealed a significant increase in time dedicated to teaching and teaching preparation except for research university faculty members. Milem et al. (2000) note, "Faculty at research universities reported a statistically nonsignificant drop in time spent on teaching" (p. 467).

Taking a global view of research university faculty members' time on task, Bentley and Kyvik (2013) looked at individual differences in faculty research time allocations across 13 countries. Their research included an examination of three key considerations: university policy of working time on research, individual motivation toward research, and family commitments. Study findings revealed individual level of interest in research was the strongest predictor of one's research time allocation even when controlling for the effects of research qualifications, previous publications, and research funding. Bentley and Kyvik reported, on average, faculty spent 18.5 hours per week engaged in research, which equated to 39% of total working hours per week. Research university faculty members employed in Germany and Argentina reported the highest time spent engaged in research at 22.5 and 21.8 hours per week, respectively. Research university faculty members in the United States reported 17.6 hours per week engaged in research, which is higher than those figures reported through the FSSE survey findings.

As evidenced by the literature presented in this chapter, research university faculty members are the most research-active faculty as compared to their peers at other institution types as discussed in the fourth through sixth chapters, which aligns with the institutional mission of research universities. However, they also spend a considerable amount of time supporting teaching at their respective institutions as evidenced by the FSSE (Indiana University, 2016) survey results (22.07 hours on teaching for lower division courses, 20.39 hours on teaching for upper division courses). Such evidence provides a counternarrative to the assumption that research university faculty members focus *only* on research when engaged in academic work.

Challenges

"Today the future of the American research university is more uncertain than it has been in the last 50 years" (Research Universities Futures Consortium, 2012, p. 9). This quotation appears in a report titled *The Current Health and Future Well-Being of the American Research University* that was prepared by the Research Universities Futures Consortium, a group of 25 of the most prominent U.S. research universities. The goal of the study was to conduct a "'bottom up'" (p. 10) evaluation of the 21st-century research university to determine the ways in which, as a collective, they could respond and contribute to the economic and social challenges while doing so in a resource-constrained environment. The concerns drawn from this consortium align with recent media coverage (Kiley, 2012b), scholarly examinations (Brint, 2005; Mohrman, Ma, & Baker, 2008; Reindl & Brower, 2001; Trow, 2001), and commencement addresses (Bowen, 2016) that highlight that research universities face major challenges, including but not limited to rapidly changing technologies, financial constraints, and global and for-profit competition.

The necessary role of technology in higher education is unmistakable. The academy was one of the early adopters of the Internet (Katzen, 2009) and has come to rely on technology to support research productivity, as well as educational program delivery. However, decreased funding at the federal and state levels has resulted in underinvestment for institutional cyber-infrastructure that affects long-term increases in innovation in research (e.g., faculty research productivity), education (e.g., program delivery), and administration (e.g., knowledge management systems) (National Research Council, 2012). Trow (2001) identified the impact of new information technologies as a high priority. "I put this first, not only because it is the most destabilizing or transforming development in higher education but also because it's implicated in all other problems higher education is facing" (p. 111).

A second challenge facing research universities is decreased funding at local, state, and national levels. Financially, research universities are tasked with managing escalating costs of higher education combined with fiscal constraints and record reductions in state and federal funding (Trow, 2001; Zusman, 2005). In his keynote address at Rutgers University's 250th anniversary presidential symposium on higher education, president emeritus of the Andrew W. Mellon Foundation William Bowen (2016) discussed the major issues facing research universities and described the present period in higher education as a time of stress and opportunity. He said, "The stress, you know all too well, derives from, first of all, shrinking resources, especially when measured on a per student basis" (para. 3). He went on to discuss other issues including higher completion rates coupled with shorter time to degree and maintaining but also improving the quality of education.

A third challenge is competition globally and from the for-profit sector, which is threatening the research university model. Schuster and Finkelstein (2006) described the rise of the research university as the central story line in 20th-century U.S. higher education. However, recent alternative forms of higher education providers are becoming more prominent, including proprietary institutions such as Argosy University, DeVry Institutes of Technology, and most notably the University of Phoenix, as well as alternative models for delivering education, including distance-learning models that employ "faculty in ways radically different from the pattern in traditional institutions"

(p. 43). Further, the globalization of economies and research systems coupled with emergent international, industrial competition have commercialized research and teaching.

Summary

Research universities continue to rely on their core competency of knowledge production as a means of responding to calls for creative solutions to the growing and increasingly complex problems facing research universities (Research Universities Futures Consortium, 2012). Although issues of functionality and productivity are better managed at the individual faculty levels, as reported by the Research Universities Futures Consortium (2012), institutional-level structures and supports are inadequate, and in some instances nonexistent, to help manage these sophisticated issues from an institutional perspective. "The result is a system that is fragmented at all levels in its approach and lacks an accepted means to rationally assess productivity and efficiency differences" (Research Universities Futures Consortium, 2012, p. 10). An understanding of the research university setting supports an examination of the scholarly learning for the faculty members employed in this institution type.

Faculty Scholarly Learning in Research Universities

The majority of research that examines the faculty experience and academic work is situated in the research university setting (Rhoades, 2007; Ward & Wolf-Wendel, 2005). These studies have shed light on the professoriate and the evolving nature of academic work. We agree with Neumann's (2009a) observation:

> In order to consider the condition and future of the academic profession, we must understand how professors' scholarly learning changes as their work and their "work worlds" (their campuses, fields of study, the academic profession) change, and as they too change as a consequence of their learning. (p. 191)

Neumann's studies (2005a, 2005b, 2009a, 2009b) laid the foundation for scholarly learning as a lens to examine the faculty experience; however, her studies were conducted on research university faculty. She recommended that future research extends this line of inquiry to other types of institutions. In the following section, we rely on Boyer's forms of scholarship to organize a discussion of faculty members' scholarly learning in research universities.

Scholarship of Discovery

Given the creation and dissemination of knowledge is the mission of the research university, it is not surprising that the majority of research about academic work in this institutional context is related to the process of engaging in the scholarship of discovery or outcomes related to the scholarship of discovery. Original research that advances knowledge and results in publications and the receipt of external grants characterize the key outcomes and are primary metrics during the promotion and tenure process (Melguizo & Strober, 2007).

Researchers have examined factors such as satisfaction, legitimacy, and intent to leave (see, for example, Bozeman & Gaughan, 2011; Gonzales, 2013; Rosser, 2004; Ryan, Healy, & Sullivan, 2012) to grasp the faculty experience in this institutional setting better. Specifically, how research active faculty members are, how their peers perceive them regarding research productivity, and the quality of contribution of that work to the institution and broader disciplinary field have been examined.

The work of Bozeman and Gaughan (2011), for example, sought to explore the experiences of tenured or tenure-track faculty members in science, technology, engineering, and mathematics (STEM) fields at a research university. Specifically, they examined job satisfaction relying on three sets of variables including the characteristics of the individual, the work context, and institutional interactions. Study findings revealed key contributors to satisfaction such as demographic characteristics, colleague interactions, and extrinsic pay motivation. The strongest predictor of job satisfaction for the faculty participants, however, was determined by departmental colleagues, particularly their perceptions of the quality of the study participants' scholarly contributions. Additionally, equitable and fair pay indicating one's value also contributed to satisfaction. Although Bozeman and Gaughan (2011) noted one aim of their research was to determine whether job satisfaction factors for university faculty members were consistent with those of other workers (which they are to some degree), they also noted the uniqueness of the tenure system and the importance of aligning incentives with performance evaluation criteria. "Our study suggests that if the 'production function' is research publications and grants, the incentives are already in alignment [for research universities]" (p. 179). Their findings support the connection between satisfaction and scholarship production, particularly in a context where such production is closely aligned with reward and incentive structures.

Engagement in the scholarship of discovery in research universities provides a clear path to gaining legitimacy in the professoriate. The work of (Gonzales, 2012, 2013; Gonzales & Terosky, 2016) has revealed that in order to earn distinction and legitimacy in the academy, particularly in research universities, faculty members must be active scholars by way of research-related activities given that is the expectation (Henderson, 2009; Terosky, 2005). However, scholars have also found such realities in liberal arts institutions where teaching and student development are critical as connected to institutional mission (Melguizo & Strober, 2007). Within the umbrella of research-related activities, certain types of scholarship are more highly regarded and privileged than others (Gonzales & Rincones, 2012).

Ryan et al. (2012) studied faculty intent to leave in research universities. Their work accounted for critical factors such as stress, satisfaction, being supported and valued, and the concept of "fit." Even within a research university setting, faculty members employed in what the authors describe as "soft-pure" disciplines (e.g., arts, humanities) were more likely to leave because such research was less highly regarded compared to applied fields. Further, workplace stress resulting from committee work, faculty meetings, bureaucratic structures, teaching load, lack of personal time, and working with underprepared students was also a contributing factor. Interestingly, increases in faculty productivity also influenced intent to leave. Increased scholarly productivity contributed to reputational gains on a broader level, thus influencing intent to leave given an increase in competitiveness and attractiveness to other more prestigious research universities.

Within the related literature of scholarship of discovery at research universities, we note that passion for one's discipline and the benefits of the scholarship of discovery for faculty members' scholarly learning are in need of further study (Neumann, 2009a,b), especially during a time of more headline-grabbing concerns discussed in this chapter.

Scholarship of Teaching

Administrators and faculty leaders at research universities have sought to create faculty development opportunities in the area of university teaching as a means of improving the quality of undergraduate education and to comprehend beliefs about teaching practices in research universities better (Kane, Sandretto, & Heath, 2002). The scholarship of teaching and learning (SoTL) is the systematic examination of teaching and learning processes that allows for public sharing and the opportunity for others to apply and assess such processes (Boyer, 1990). Examples of SoTL in research universities might include a micro-teaching workshop hosted by a center for teaching and learning, which involves collaborative course planning, peer observation of teaching, and postobservation debrief and assessment. In the context of research universities, the view of teaching and learning particularly related to undergraduate education is not a positive one. "We need to focus much more attention on undergraduate education, and we need to deliver it more effectively than we have been doing" (Rawlings, 2012, para. 20). The relative value of teaching in research universities is also in question.

Research by Fairweather (2005) illustrated the disparity in incentives related to academic work. He researched whether faculty pay reflected the push for greater commitment to teaching and learning. His findings revealed that increased attention to teaching (e.g., spending more hours per week on teaching), related to lower basic salary for faculty members in research, doctoral, and comprehensive universities. Further, faculty members employed at LACs experienced a negative factor in pay for hours spent in the classroom. A summary of findings revealed "that publishing productivity continued as a significant positive factor in pay at all types of institutions" whereas "teaching remains a negative factor in pay" (p. 417). Such realities create challenges for engaging in and the study of teaching and learning in research universities.

The majority of research about the scholarship of teaching features institutional case studies, with the exception of a volume that provides information about the scholarship on teaching as well as teaching pedagogy in research universities—*The Scholarship of Teaching and Learning in Higher Education: Contributions of Research Universities,* edited by Becker and Andrews (2010). The volume offers resources, case studies, and models of teaching and learning, campus support structures of teaching and learning, advice and guidance on how, and in what ways, teaching and learning can be incorporated more deliberately into student research and other experiential activities, and the role research universities can play as models of assessment and innovation in undergraduate education.

Examples of institutional case studies of teaching and learning in research universities include the work of Wright (2005) and Frost and Teodorescu (2001). Wright (2005), for example, relied on survey data from over 2,600 faculty members at a large, top-ranked public research university to examine the congruence in faculty beliefs about teaching at a research university. Findings revealed that teaching networks permeated more vastly in congruent units in which more cross-departmental interactions related to teaching occurred, thus facilitating opportunities to discuss teaching practices, values related to teaching, and definitions (and agreement) of what effective teaching was. As Wright (2005) noted, "in selected contexts, shaped by opportunities for social interaction, [research university] faculty can develop a sense that the value they accord to teaching and the ways they define 'good teaching' are congruent with their department" (p. 347).

Frost and Teodorescu (2001) also identified the need for research universities to "rehabilitate the status of teaching" (p. 397), and their research provided details on the systematic approach campus leaders and administrators at Emory University employed to achieve a better balance between teaching and research. Emory created a faculty commission on teaching to "examine the most critical issues concerning the support and improvement of teaching and to make specific recommendations for improvement" (p. 400). Key action items were identified to support teaching at Emory such as improving teaching evaluations, increasing faculty development opportunities related to teaching, and the need to improve physical infrastructures related to teaching. The work of Wright (2005) and Frost and Teodorescu (2001) makes an important contribution in that it sheds light on the examination of teaching and learning practices in research universities, highlights the importance of facilitating dialogue among colleagues about effective teaching, and identifies areas of opportunity related to teaching as a means of improving processes within and across departments and academic units.

What is missing from this line of inquiry, however, is an examination of research university faculty members engaging in the study of teaching, rather than a movement across research universities to improve undergraduate teaching practices (Frost & Teodorescu, 2001; Wright, 2005). As evidenced by the research of Terosky (2005), few professors at major research universities engaged in research about teaching resulting in publications about the scholarship of teaching in their respective fields. Findings revealed that the faculty participants were supported in their scholarship of teaching work as long as they were also upholding their scholarship of discovery in their disciplinary areas.

In sum, the institutional case studies presented here illustrate that administrators and campus leaders are seeking to improve undergraduate teaching effectiveness in this institutional setting. Further, research university faculty members engage in discussions and disseminate resources about improved teaching practices. Far less research about the faculty experience in research universities, however, delves into the inquiry and study of teaching and learning or examines the process by which research university faculty members engage in the scholarship of teaching (exception Terosky, 2005). One such explanation is linked to the work of Fairweather (2005), in which he revealed that research excellence, or rather engagement in traditional research, is still more highly valued in academic work across institution types.

Scholarship of Engagement

The scholarship of engagement looks beyond the actual service duties of faculty members and instead focuses on the rigor and application of disciplinary expertise with results that can be shared with and/or evaluated by peers (Boyer, 1990). Examples of the scholarship of engagement supported by research universities might include community partnerships aimed at supporting economic development. Scholars have explored the scholarship of engagement from institutional (e.g., administrator) and individual faculty members' perspectives (O'Meara 2002, 2005a).

The Academy for Global Engagement (AGE) Fellowship Program at Michigan State University is one such example of the scholarship of engagement. AGE is creating a new generation of international research experts at Michigan State University by offering faculty an innovative opportunity to expand their scholarship on a global level. The College of Agriculture and Natural Resources (CANR) and the College of Engineering (CoE) seek to address global challenges such as hunger and malnutrition, health issues, access to clean water, and low-cost energy solutions. Through the Academy of Global Engagement Fellowship Program, CANR and CoE seek to develop the next generation of visionary researchers who can anticipate the needs of the global world and continuously support Michigan State University's land-grant mission on an international level (http://www.globalacademy.msu.edu/).

The scholarship of engagement is also considered an important and relevant form of scholarship for historically Black colleges and universities (HBCUs) given their mission and past commitments (Lowe, 2008; Marshall et al., 2016; Sydnor, Hawkins, & Edwards, 2010). According to Lowe (2008) "for HBCU faculty members engaged in scholarship, much of it follows a historical tradition of being public—responding to problems and opportunities in their respective communities through such forms as direct service, technical assistance and the dissemination of reports" (p. 551). Yet, Lowe also noted "the majority of HBCUs involved in university-community partnerships are not major research institutions" (p. 551). Jackson State University is one of 10 HBCUs classified as Research Universities (U.S. Department of Education, 2015). Of those 10 HBCUs, five are Higher Research Activity (R2), and five are Moderate Research Activity (R3).

Lowe (2008) highlighted the role of Jackson State University's (JSU) Department of Urban and Regional Planning (DURP) faculty in the e-City Initiative. The e-City Initiative intended an all-inclusive approach to community revitalization and economic development with the assistance of technology. In addition to successfully securing funding from the Fannie Mae Foundation, DURP faculty were extensively involved in the planning, data collection and analysis, and presentation of findings for this project. Unfortunately, although faculty were awarded release time to participate in this university–community partnership, which was initially advanced by the new JSU president, their role in the e-City initiative was not recognized in the promotion and tenure process (Lowe, 2008).

In addition to institutional programs, researchers have explored the scholarship of engagement in research university settings. O'Meara (2002), for example, conducted case studies of institutions that put in place new promotion and tenure policies to broaden the definition of scholarship. She interviewed faculty, administrators, and promotion and tenure committee members to understand the values and beliefs influencing the assessment of engaged scholarship specifically. She found that institutional type, mission, and focus shaped faculty assessment of engaged scholarship as much, if not more than new policy language. Faculty who became involved in engaged scholarship did so despite having been socialized to do more traditional disciplinary work. The faculty members most heavily involved in the scholarship of engagement often felt marginalized on their respective campuses. Despite policy language reform noting the importance of and need to expand the definition of scholarship, there remained clear evaluation and reward structures favoring a more traditional view of scholarship.

O'Meara (2005b) also conducted a national survey of chief academic officers (CAOs), to understand the degree to which campuses put in place promotion and tenure policy reform as suggested by Boyer's (1990) book, *Scholarship Reconsidered: Priorities of the Professoriate*. The sample represented all 4-year institution types (e.g., institution types including doctoral/research, master's, and baccalaureate institutions). Fifty percent of 4-year institutions were represented in the final study sample. Two thirds of the CAOs surveyed reported reforms on their respective campuses to encourage multiple forms of scholarship. Institutions that implemented reforms found that engagement and teaching scholarship counted more for tenure and promotion than it had before they put in place promotion and tenure language reform. However, institutional context also mattered; the more research-oriented institutions still reported traditional criteria mattered more in the assessment of scholarship, even if some change had occurred to regard newer forms of scholarship better.

To summarize, faculty members who are active in the scholarship of engagement provide an important service to their respective institutions and surrounding communities in which their efforts seek to support. Despite rhetoric of the importance of the scholarship of engagement, faculty members active in this way feel marginalized. Further, policy and practice are still lagging behind in research-oriented institutions regarding recognizing this important contribution or opportunity to support (and acknowledge) faculty learning.

Scholarship of Integration

The scholarship of integration is the synthesis of knowledge across disciplines/fields, topics within a given discipline, or across time (Boyer, 1990). One of the primary ways in which the scholarship of integration is realized is through interdisciplinary collaboration and research teams. Such collaboration is inherent in STEM fields, for example, given the cross-disciplinary work that spans scientific boundaries. In research universities, the process and outcomes of the scholarship of integration are often situated in research centers, typically interdisciplinary in nature, given they bring together scholars from diverse fields to work on pressing national and disciplinary problems (Formicola, 2007; Sá, 2008).

Faculty learning that results from the scholarship of integration has received much less attention in the literature as compared to the other forms of scholarship in research universities given the associated challenges—specifically organizational structures that favor the academic department and discipline, and academic research journals that favor pure disciplinary work (Jacobs, 2014). Interdisciplinarity is a virtue in higher education, yet has been described as a "risky route" (Byrne, 2014, n.p.). As Sá (2008) noted, although there is no shortage of external encouragement for faculty members to engage in interdisciplinary research, the organizational structures are insufficient (or nonexistent is some instances) given the building blocks of the discipline and academic departments. In fact, research universities are ripe with disincentives to deviate from disciplinary, departmental forms (Abbott, 2001), and those messages are communicated as early as the PhD experience creating barriers and challenges for doctoral students pursuing interdisciplinary courses of study (Holley, 2009, 2015).

These institutional disincentives were acknowledged in the work of Lattuca (2001). In her apt assessment, she noted that as disciplines become more complex, so too do the scholars who engage in corresponding community practices as they seek to contribute new knowledge within their disciplinary and departmental domains. Such realities broaden the relationships, as disciplinary and departmental members move from a more tight-knit community to more distal relationships (Lattuca, 2001). These changes, coupled with the growth of new knowledge over the past century "have moved interdisciplinarity from the academic periphery to a more central scholarly location" (p.3). Although these opportunities and challenges are relevant for all institution types, the reward and incentive structures in research universities make engaging in the scholarship of integration complex, despite calls for "cutting-edge research" and "scholarly innovations" that align with the goals of integration. There is a larger body of literature on interdisciplinarity (Creamer & Lattuca, 2005; Lattuca, 2001), team science (Cooke, Gorman, Duran, & Taylor, 2007), and research collaboration (Lee, 2000; Van Rijnsoever & Hessels, 2011) as well as the associated outcomes of those collaborations as measured through faculty productivity (Gulbrandsen & Smeby, 2005; Lee, 2000). Faculty scholarly learning, as a result of engagement in the scholarship of integration, is not a typical outcome of interest.

In conclusion, although research and practice of the faculty experience situate that work predominantly in the research university setting, few scholars examine the scholarly learning of faculty members as they engage in all areas of academic work. Despite the rhetoric in which teaching, interdisciplinarity, and service are valued, the research presented in this chapter has highlighted the institutional realities and hurdles that limit engagement in areas beyond the scholarship of discovery. To that end, we discuss the barriers and opportunities in research universities related to the scholarly learning of their faculties.

Barriers to Scholarly Learning in Research Universities

As Kuh and Hu (2001) noted, "Research universities enjoy the highest status among colleges and universities" (p. 1), yet they are not without their challenges and critics. Although we believe the creation and dissemination of new knowledge meet both an institutional and societal need, such a narrow focus (and corresponding reward and incentive structures) hinders the types and depth of scholarly learning encouraged and supported for the faculty members employed at research universities. In the following section, three challenges to scholarly learning in research universities are discussed: the discrepancy between what is valued versus what is rewarded, increased competition and demands for productivity, and academic capitalism.

Valued Versus Rewarded

The predominant focus of research and practice of the faculty experience at research universities is centered on the scholarship of discovery as an activity that supports intent to stay (or leave) or as a source of satisfaction as discussed earlier in this chapter. Despite the institutional case studies presented in this chapter in which teaching was explored as a critical component of academic work, research by Fairweather (2005) examined faculty salary related to engagement in teaching versus research revealing that time spent in the classroom is less valued than time spent engaged in research, regardless of institution type. Such a reward and evaluation system neglects what Åkerlind (2005) described as a holistic view of all the areas in which growth and development can occur in the professoriate. Such a narrow focus fails to adequately portray faculty life in a 21st-century research university despite calls for greater efforts toward undergraduate teaching. Teaching and related activities are significant for faculty members in research universities (Indiana University, 2016), yet a greater emphasis is placed on research and the scholarship of discovery. The disconnect between what is valued and rewarded in a research university setting contributes to the next challenge—increased demands for competition and productivity.

Increased Demands for Competition and Productivity

In their study of grassroots faculty leadership, Kezar and Lester (2009) sought to explore the factors that supported and inhibited grassroots faculty leadership (and the corresponding development) beyond formal academic leadership roles (e.g., department chair). As part of their discussion of the barriers, Kezar and Lester (2009) discussed the increasing publication standards for promotion and tenure. "Prolific publishers have gone from one in nine to one in four of the faculty since 1969 ... the pressure to publish has risen significantly" (p. 718). Increased standards for publication result in fewer efforts placed toward other areas of academic work such as teaching, service, and formal and informal leadership.

Along with the rise in publication standards, regarding both quantity and quality, the research university environment has become "hypercompetitive and complex" (Research Universities Futures Consortium, 2012, p. 28). As noted by the Research Universities Futures Consortium (2012), research is one of the most complex aspects of higher education that is very much influenced by resources, or lack thereof. A key finding of their report noted, "Unsustainable costs for some universities and corrosive hypercompetition between universities have serious consequences, impacting the ability of faculty to be successful researchers in the present and reducing student interest in research careers" (p. 28). The report noted that such competition is not just between institutions but even within institutions related to academic work and roles (e.g., teaching versus research), department versus department, and discipline versus discipline (e.g., science versus humanities). Such competition creates challenges and barriers to effective collaboration and greatly hinders opportunities for faculty scholarly learning beyond the scholarship of discovery.

Academic Capitalism

Academic capitalism is the trend for faculty members to subsidize their salary with grants and other external sources of funding and contracts. As a framework, academic capitalism allows researchers and practitioners to understand higher education's shift from creating scholarship and learning as a public good to knowledge production as a commodity to be monetized by the market (Cantwell, Kauppinen, & Slaughter, 2014). The result: faculty members are more independent and self-directed, thus creating the ability to make supplemental income and profit from their research (Slaughter & Rhoades, 2004). According to Kezar and Lester (2009), academic capitalism permeates science fields and research universities predominantly but affects all sectors and institution types in U.S. higher education.

Opportunities for Scholarly Learning in Research Universities

Despite the challenges noted, research universities are ripe with opportunities to support (and properly reward and acknowledge) the scholarly learning of their faculties across a range of experiences and academic work roles. In the process, we believe those opportunities can involve partnerships and collaborations with key stakeholders within and outside of the academy. We argue that faculty engagement in high-impact practices such as undergraduate research, increasing opportunities for collaboration with internal and external stakeholders, and fostering service to institutions as a means of encouraging scholarly learning are a few of key opportunities for research universities.

Scholarly Learning Through High-Impact Practices

Kuh and Hu (2001) noted that educational enterprises, specifically research universities, that support reward systems that favor scholarly productivity over high-quality undergraduate teaching and advising discourage meaningful intellectual engagement at the undergraduate student level. Supporting students in high-impact practices creates opportunities to support the scholarly learning of faculty that spans the forms of scholarship that Boyer characterized.

Although research shows that most faculty members mentor students in undergraduate research (UR) experiences mostly through organizational citizenship behaviors (Eagan, Sharkness, Hurtado, Mosqueda, & Chang, 2011), researchers have revealed critical outcomes for faculty mentors of undergraduate research such as personal satisfaction, fulfillment, rejuvenation, networking, friendship and support, and reputational gains for talent development (Johnson, 2007). Administrators and campus leaders have directed tangible resources and rewards to undergraduate researchers, scholars, and artists (e.g., summer stipends and housing), yet have neglected to do so at the faculty level, thus failing to recognize the faculty mentors whose intellectual and affective labor are paramount to supporting undergraduate research experiences (Baker, Greer, Lunsford, Pifer, & Ihas, 2016). Administrators and campus leaders have an opportunity to create the appropriate reward and incentive structures to acknowledge engagement in UR, thus facilitating the scholarly learning of faculty members in concert with undergraduate students.

Increasing Opportunities for Collaboration with Internal and External Stakeholders

In her work, Creamer (2005) initiated a call to action within the academy to explicitly acknowledge, value, and reward collaboration and coauthorship. She argued, "The absence of explicit references to collaboration in texts about faculty evaluation is a clear acknowledgment of the individualistic values that underlie the traditional academic reward structure" (p. 86). By promoting and rewarding such efforts, research universities can more explicitly support internal and external collaborations as a means of encouraging scholarly learning beyond the scholarship of discovery.

For instance, the work of Mohrman et al. (2008) featured what they referred to as the Emerging Global Model. This model was conceived by a group of scholars, the New Century Scholars, from around the globe whose efforts (and reputation) represent cutting-edge research while also embracing the forces of globalization. "These top universities look beyond the boundaries of the countries in which they are located to define their scope as trans-national in nature. Their peers span the globe" (p. 6). Such networks facilitate the sharing of best practices while also creating built in collaborations and sharing of social capital.

Institutional Service to Support Scholarly Learning

Service is part of the traditional academic workload yet carries the least weight concerning promotion and tenure, regardless of institution type (Tierney & Bensimon, 1996; Ward, 2003). Given the mission of knowledge production, research university administrators, campus leaders, and faculty members have an opportunity to connect service responsibilities to community initiatives and outreach to support scholarly learning.

In their research, Neumann and Terosky (2007) studied recently tenured faculty members in four U.S. research universities with the guiding belief that service expectations and engagement increase at this career stage. The goal was to understand what forms such service took and the associated developmental gains. Study participants described their service experiences as expanding and intensifying in the level of importance, as believed to occur for the midcareer faculty members. They also described the transformation such service took and discussed an increase in more service engagements. Although their research did not specifically examine the scholarship of engagement, but rather traditional service to institution, some study participants did engage in and share their experiences within the scholarship of engagement. Within these changes, study participants talked about the learning they experienced, particularly related to the complementary nature service can have with research and teaching.

Conclusion and Implications

Research universities maintain an important position in the U.S. higher education landscape. Known for cultivating and disseminating cutting-edge research, it is no surprise that the majority of research and practice about the faculty experience aligns with the reward and incentive structures in this institution type through a focus on the scholarship of discovery. However, this focus neglects the reality of time allocation studies of research university faculty members and the environmental forces that affect all aspects of academic work in this institutional context. We see opportunities for faculty members and administrators to bring the focus back to scholarly learning and to think creatively about the ways in which policy and practice can support such efforts.

We urge administrators to think about and articulate institutional mission and values in concrete ways as a means of highlighting the important role research universities have maintained and continue to maintain in the higher education landscape—knowledge creation and dissemination. Such articulation supports conversations with faculty members as both stakeholder groups think about the role of mission and values as connected to institutional, divisional, departmental, and programmatic initiatives. Such collaboration and connection helps to align institutional goals and priorities with individual outcomes and needs. Rather than have these aspects operate on parallel tracks (with academic capitalism as the resulting by-product), they can work together to better serve the institution and the individuals employed in this institutional setting by refocusing efforts around mission and values and a rearticulation of how the mission and values can be realized across Boyer's forms of scholarship. These conversations serve as an important foundation to creating deliberate linkages with internal and external networks, which we argue is a strategic advantage of research universities given the goals of knowledge creation and dissemination.

The next chapter features faculty scholarly learning in comprehensive universities.

Comprehensive Colleges and Universities

THE SCHOLARLY LEARNING of faculty members employed at comprehensive colleges and universities is the focus of this chapter. We first define comprehensive colleges and universities and outline the roles and responsibilities of their full-time faculty members. Key themes on the scholarly learning of faculty members at comprehensive colleges and universities are offered, followed by a discussion of barriers and supports.

Defining Comprehensives and Their Students and Faculty

Defining comprehensive colleges and universities is not an easy task because numerous labels, categories, and definitions abound about this institutional type. Some of the labels or categories applied include comprehensive universities, state comprehensive universities, regional public universities, regional universities, or master's colleges or universities (M1, M2, M3). In the updated Carnegie Classification (Carnegie Classification of Institutions of Higher Education, 2015), comprehensive colleges and universities span several sectors, with the majority falling under the category of Master's Colleges and Universities and Baccalaureate Colleges–Diverse Fields. With the various labels, categories, and definitions available, scholars, practitioners, and public stakeholders often use these terms interchangeably, thereby adding a level of inconsistency in regard to appropriate labels and definitions. For the purpose of consistency in this chapter, comprehensive colleges and universities are defined as:

> *a public or private 4-year institution that offers a range of degree programs, including baccalaureates, master's degrees, and a small number of professional doctorates (e.g., business, education), with less than 50% of the degrees falling under liberal arts disciplines; comprehensive colleges and universities emphasize professional and career preparation and attention to regional needs.*

Mission

Historically, comprehensive colleges and universities have been grounded in teaching ("normal") colleges, technical colleges, HBCUs, MSIs, and branch campuses with a mission to provide access to higher education for underserved populations (e.g., first-generation students, veterans), offer vocationally or professionally oriented degrees (e.g., education, industrial careers), and serve regional needs (Bardo, 1990; Geiger, 2005). Based on these traditions, historians argue that comprehensives "more deserve to be known as the People's Universities than do the land grant institutions" (Henderson, 2011, p. 37). More recently, other types of institutions have "moved toward a more applied and vocational orientation," thereby resulting in an "encroachment" on comprehensives' "distinctiveness of mission" (Henderson, 2009, pp. 6–7).

Despite its prevalence in U.S. higher education, comprehensive colleges and universities have been called "the forgotten colleges of America" (Henderson & Kane, 1991, p. 340; see also Thelin, 2004) because they have been mostly understudied (Grubb & Lazerson, 2005; Henderson, 2011; Wolf-Wendel & Ward, 2006). This lack of study of comprehensives is particularly alarming in light of the fact that they enroll a large percentage of college students in the United States and they have been expanding their enrollment and program offerings at "unprecedented rates since World War II" (Tang & Chamberlain, 2003, p. 104). Based on the 2015 summary presented by the Carnegie Classification of Institutions of Higher Education, more than 1,000 of the more than 4,500 public and nonprofit institutions of higher education are comprehensives (399 Master's Colleges and Universities–Large

Programs, 215 Master's Colleges and Universities–Medium Programs, 145 Master's Colleges and Universities–Small Programs, 325 Baccalaureate-Diverse Fields). Besides descriptors such as expanding student enrollments and programs, comprehensives are also characterized by their "variety and variability" (Henderson, 2009, p. 7) in terms of range in size (small to large), geographic location (rural to urban), and selectivity rates (mid to low).

Students

Comprehensives grant about half of all bachelor's and master's degrees in the United States (Soo, 2011). According to the National Center for Education Statistics (NCES, 2007), a third of students enrolled in all public 4-year colleges/universities are enrolled in comprehensives. In the 2015 Carnegie Classification of Institutions of Higher Education summary, comprehensives enrolled the following percentages of the total enrollment of students: 16.3% Master's Colleges and Universities–Large Programs, 3.9% Master's Colleges and Universities–Medium Programs, 1.8% Master's Colleges and Universities–Small Programs, and 2.7% Baccalaureate-Diverse Fields.

Comprehensive students traditionally are first-generation college students pursuing practice-oriented programs and degrees, often in education or other professional fields (Grubb & Lazerson, 2005). Today, comprehensives face a tension between their historical commitment to access and the desire to increase their status by attracting prepared students via honors colleges and programs and research programs (Henderson, 2009). However, when compared to research universities and selective LACs, comprehensives are not viewed as high-status institutions, essentially because of notions of legitimacy around selectivity rates and overall competitiveness with more highly selective institutions, but also as a result of comprehensives' philosophical commitment to providing access to higher education for a broad range of students with varying levels of preparation for college-level work (Henderson, 2009).

Faculty

At the faculty level, fairly little is known about the experiences of faculty members who do not work at well-resourced research universities or elite, private liberal arts colleges (Dougherty, 2011; Schuster & Finkelstein, 2006), which

TABLE 2
FSSE Time Allocation, Hours per Week, in Comprehensives

	Comprehensive Lower Division Courses	Comprehensive Upper Division Courses
Teaching	21.72	21.75
Advising	4.3	6.20
Research	6.98	8.04
Service	6.35	9.06
TOTALS	**39.35**	**45.05**

Note: These figures include Master's L, M, S categories and Baccalaureate Diversity

is alarming because a third of full-time faculty employed at 4-year institutions in 2003 were employed at comprehensive universities (NCES, 2003). The National Center for Education Statistics (2003) found that comprehensives and research universities have a similar number of doctoral-trained faculty. This results in a tension for most comprehensive faculty members, one where the experience of graduate education through the lens of the major research university model contrasts with their academic roles and expectations in the context of working at a comprehensive (Henderson, 2011; Terosky & Gonzales, 2016).

According to FSSE (Indiana University, 2016) results, comprehensive faculty who teach lower division courses spend, on average, 21.72 hours per week engaged in teaching and related activities, 4.30 hours advising students, 6.98 hours engaged in research efforts, and 6.35 hours conducting campus and community service for a total of 39.35 hours per week. Comprehensive faculty who teach upper division courses teach, on average, 21.75 hours a week, spend 6.20 hours on advising students, 8.04 hours engaged in research efforts, and 9.06 hours conducting service activities for a total of 45.05 hours per week (see Table 2). Typically, the teaching loads of faculty members employed by comprehensives is double that of research universities (Henderson, 2009).

Challenges

Comprehensive colleges and universities face a plethora of challenges in the 21st century. Faculty are called on to increasingly perform a variety of tasks, many of which are contradictory in nature (e.g., publish more yet be available to students at all times) (Henderson, 2007, 2011). This request is often referred to as being asked to do "more with less." One of these tasks, a task that was not originally a core focus of the comprehensive mission, is research productivity. Comprehensive institutions are increasingly placing greater value on research productivity in their promotion and tenure processes, as well as in their less formal means of valuing faculty work (O'Meara, 2007). Critics of this trend argue that increased pressure to publish, while also upholding the core of the comprehensive mission of teaching and service, has resulted in confusion as to what the institution prioritizes and what makes it unique from other institution types (Henderson, 2009, 2011). This process, referred to as striving institutions (O'Meara, 2007) or "mission confusion" (Henderson, 2009, p. 13) is examined in greater detail later in this chapter and is considered one of the paramount challenges facing comprehensives: how to achieve status while serving their region and students (Henderson, 2009).

In sum, comprehensive colleges and universities are public or private 4-year institutions that offer a range of degree programs, including baccalaureates, master's degrees, and a small number of professional doctorates (e.g., business, education), with the historic mission of emphasizing professional preparation, student-centered education, and regional needs. Although comprehensives are widespread in the U.S. higher education landscape and growing at significant rates, an inadequate level of attention from the government and research sectors has been paid to this institutional type. Moreover, a significant pressure has been placed on comprehensive faculty as they strive to uphold the mission of student-centered education in professional preparation and regional needs while also increasingly being called on to emulate the research productivity of colleagues at more research-oriented institutions.

Faculty Scholarly Learning at Comprehensives

What does faculty scholarly learning look like at comprehensives? When considering both the institutional and individual influences on faculty work and decisions, the answer to this question is a complex one. As such, the recent literature on faculty scholarly learning at comprehensives pushes back on a "one-size-fits-all" approach and instead, highlights that comprehensive faculty engage in the full range of Boyer's (1990) four forms of scholarship described in the second chapter of this monograph (i.e., scholarships of discovery, teaching, engagement, and integration). Work by Park and Braxton (2013) that studied 4,000 tenure-track or nontenure-track faculty members at four institution types (i.e., research universities, doctoral universities, comprehensive universities, and baccalaureate colleges, selectivity I and selectivity II) and four academic disciplines (i.e., biology, chemistry, history, and sociology) found that 81.6% of their faculty participants engaged in more than one form of Boyer's scholarship. In addition, Terosky and Gonzales (2016) studied 50 faculty members employed at open or broad access or regional institutions, finding that scholarly learning, defined as knowledge expansion and knowledge creation, was taking place in a variety of ways and with a diverse set of outcomes. Terosky and Gonzales highlighted how some of their comprehensive faculty shifted from focusing on their success as a researcher to the development of their students' learning through the scholarship of teaching, whereas others pursued the scholarship of engagement by collaborating on a community-related project, and others found success in publishing in their traditional, disciplinary journals (i.e., scholarship of discovery).

In addition to pushing back on a "one-size-fits-all" approach to scholarly learning, recent literature emphasizes that personal fulfillment and public obligation are particularly fitting concepts for comprehensive faculty in light of their passions for their disciplinary expertise as well as their obligations to their institutions' regional needs. Drawing on the metaphor of a crossroads of personal fulfillment and public obligation presented by Hansen (1994, 1995), Terosky and Gonzales (2016) discussed the significance of honoring both the personal fulfillment and the public obligation that propel faculty scholarly learning and activity, especially at institutional contexts like comprehensive colleges and universities. Similarly, Neumann (2009a) argued that scholarly learning is a "beacon of meaning in [faculty] careers and lives," (p. 224) and therefore calls on higher educational stakeholders to remain open to the various ways faculty members engage in scholarly learning and the varied supports needed to facilitate that learning.

In sum, the recent literature is reframing commonly held assumptions about scholarship taking place at only research universities or other well-resourced institutions. Instead, this strand of literature is pushing back on the "one size fits all" for faculty learning, specifically by connecting individuals' disciplinary passions/personal fulfillment and public obligations (Gonzales & Terosky, 2016; Hansen, 1994, 1995; Neumann, 2009a; Terosky & Gonzales, 2016). The following section examines how the different forms of scholarly learning, per Boyer's framework, play out in the comprehensive context.

Scholarship of Discovery

The scholarship of discovery, defined as traditional, disciplinary research, is increasingly being encouraged at comprehensive universities, largely because of the phenomenon of "striving institutions" or "mission creep" that has been evolving since the 1970s (Morphew, 2002; O'Meara, 2007). Striving is when lower ranked institutions emulate higher ranked colleges and universities, typically resulting heightened expectations for faculty to conduct and publish discipline-specific research, often at the expense of teaching or service (Henderson, 2007, 2011; O'Meara, 2007). Comprehensive colleges and universities are particularly vulnerable to striving because of their lower status in the academic hierarchy (Morphew, 2002; O'Meara, 2007). Scholars of this phenomenon outline common actions followed by striving institutions, including (a) hiring faculty members with training and philosophical dispositions geared toward research, (b) promoting "cosmopolitan" perspectives that emphasize external and disciplinary constituencies rather than loyalty to local communities and employing institutions, and (c) aligning promotion, tenure, and financial awards to higher expectations for research (Morphew, 2002; O'Meara, 2007; Youn & Price, 2009).

The extant literature has documented that striving, notably rising research and publishing expectations, is occurring at all institution types, including comprehensive colleges and universities. A study comparing faculty surveys between 1972 to 1992 found that faculty from all types of institutions reported a rise in publishing expectations and the largest proportional rise was noted by comprehensive faculty members (Youn & Price, 2009). Faculty surveys by the Carnegie Foundation for the Advancement of Teaching found that the percentage of comprehensive faculty who strongly agreed that it was difficult to achieve tenure without publications rose from 6% to 43% between 1960 and 1989 (Boyer, 1990).

Henderson (2011) warned against overemphasizing publication rates for comprehensive faculty. Following an analysis of publishing patterns by faculty employed at all types of institutions from the 1960s to the current day, Henderson (2011) found that although publication rates have risen for all faculty, state comprehensive university faculty's publishing rates remain low in absolute numbers when compared to major research universities and LACs and likely do not "generate very much visibility or prestige" (p. 56). Henderson (2009, 2011) also found that comprehensive faculty members' publishing rates and acquisition of basic research funds from the federal government continued to fall below the rates of faculty members at major research universities. Similarly, Toutkoushian, Porter, Danielson, and Hollis (2003) studied publication rates in the Institute for Scientific Information Index and found that comprehensive university faculty were outpublished by research university faculty by a ratio of 20 to 1 (see also Braxton et al., 2002). Comprehensives "that have attempted to mimic the research universities," noted Henderson (2009), "have failed to do so or have fallen short of what they could have been" (p. 186; see also Henderson & Kane, 1991). As such, Henderson (2009) warns that state comprehensive universities jeopardize their historic identity around teaching and regional service for an ever-elusive quest for status through publishing. In agreement, despite calls for a broader view of scholarship, scholars have not concluded whether this has influenced a deemphasis on traditional research activities and publishing expectations at comprehensive colleges and universities (O'Meara, 2005a, 2005b).

In sum, comprehensive institutions are increasingly striving for greater productivity in the realm of scholarship of discovery by its faculty, yet critics argue that current rates of publication of traditional research lag among comprehensive faculty when compared to their peers at more research-oriented institutions.

Scholarship of Teaching

Building on the seminal work of Boyer (1990), higher education scholars argue that the scholarship of teaching, defined as researching and applying pedagogical methods and sharing findings with colleagues, might be particularly relevant to comprehensive faculty members' research agendas and their institutions' teaching missions (Boyer, 1990; Henderson & Buchanan, 2007). Historically, publications in journals dedicated to the SoTL have been rewarded at comprehensives (Henderson, 2009). However, Henderson (2009) also explains:

> *Scholarship of teaching publications might also be seen as proxies for good teaching, although to date there is no evidence that those who engage in the scholarship of teaching are better teachers for doing so, or even that work in the scholarship of teaching has improved college teaching. (pp. 17–18; see also McKinney, 2006)*

Studies on comprehensive faculty members' engagement in the scholarship of teaching offer somewhat contradictory views. A study conducted by Braxton, Luckey, and Helland (2006) found no institutional differences in the scholarship of teaching publication activity across all institution types. In contrast, Henderson and Buchanan (2007) studied publication trends across four pedagogical journals representing the disciplines of sociology, chemistry, psychology, and marketing and found that comprehensive or baccalaureate faculty members rarely published in research-oriented journals,. They did, however, publish articles in pedagogical journals at a significantly higher rate (.50 for doctoral authors, .37 for comprehensive university authors, and .13 for baccalaureate authors). Henderson and Buchanan (2007) also found that state comprehensive university faculty members are increasingly involved in leadership roles on editorial boards for journals dedicated to the scholarship of teaching. Work by Terosky and Gonzales (2016) found that many of their comprehensive participants parlayed their inquiry skills, honed through graduate schools and traditional research, to advance the learning of others (namely their students), specifically by facilitating critical thinking and undergraduate and graduate research opportunities.

The scholarship of teaching, in summary, has been rewarded among comprehensive faculty in the past and research on trends in the scholarship of teaching at the comprehensive level, albeit contradictory at times, indicates that this scholarship and leadership pathway is used by comprehensive faculty.

Scholarship of Engagement

The scholarship of engagement, defined as the use of ideas from one's discipline for solving problems, is also considered a significant form of scholarship for faculty employed in comprehensives because of the institution's historical commitment to regional needs. "In an era when the need for expertise in business, education, government, and social services is well recognized," wrote Henderson (2009), "[state comprehensive university] faculty members who are willing to apply their expertise can provide major public service" (pp. 9–10). In agreement, Soo (2011) asserted that regional stewardship, a commitment to contributing to and "being of a particular region," is a "specific role that regional comprehensive universities can play, perhaps a unique role that no other institution in society can play" (p. 7). Like the scholarship of teaching, studies contradict whether or not comprehensive faculty members are more likely to conduct research related to the scholarship of engagement. One study conducted by Braxton et al. (2006) found that comprehensive faculty reported fewer scholarship of engagement publications than their research and doctoral university colleagues and equal publications to their liberal arts colleagues. Others, such as Henderson (2009), explain that research at comprehensives, especially state-funded comprehensives, typically leads to products associated with the scholarship of engagement, for example technical studies and/or evaluation reports for regional businesses, schools, and agencies. Owing to their regional and practitioner nature, these scholarly products are often difficult to distribute within scholarly or traditional publication mediums (Henderson, 2009).

In sum, scholars note that the scholarship of engagement is a significant pathway for comprehensive faculty members because of the institutional commitment to applying scholarly expertise to regional needs. Studies on levels of productivity in the scholarship of engagement are inconclusive because the measures of scholarship of engagement products face challenges in measurement.

Scholarship of Integration

Recent literature suggests that the scholarship of integration, defined as synthesizing knowledge across disciplines, across topics within a discipline, or across time (Boyer, 1990), is an area of interest for comprehensive faculty members. Park and Braxton (2013) studied 4,000 tenure-track or nontenure-track faculty members at four institution types (i.e., research universities, doctoral universities, comprehensive universities, and baccalaureate LACs, selectivity I, and selectivity II) and four academic disciplines (i.e., biology, chemistry, history, and sociology). They found that their comprehensive faculty participants participated greatly in activities associated with a category they labeled, "Scholars of Dissemination." Scholars of Dissemination blend the scholarships of integration and teaching by engaging in the following types of scholarly activities: "trying a new instructional practice, publishing a review of literature on an interdisciplinary topic, publishing a book chapter applying theory from outside the home discipline, publishing a new instructional method, and publishing an approach for class management" (p. 322). Based on this list of activities, Scholars of Dissemination follow cosmopolitan (serving external reference groups) and local (serving internal reference groups at their institution or in their region) orientations.

The scholarship of integration, to summarize, is considered a significant interest of comprehensive faculty, particularly in light of interest in disseminating scholarship, although the limited studies in this area call for further research.

Summary of Faculty Scholarly Learning in Comprehensives

In conclusion, the literature on comprehensive faculty members' scholarly learning highlights several themes, albeit at times contradictory results. One theme is that scholars emphasize that comprehensive faculty are both consumers of knowledge, or "consummatory scholarship" in the words of Henderson (2009, p. 19), as well as producers of knowledge. As producers of knowledge, comprehensive faculty engage in multiple forms of scholarship, per Boyer's framework (1990), including the scholarships of teaching, engagement, integration, and discovery. There are some contradictions among scholars as to whether or not comprehensive faculty members engage more heavily in different forms of scholarship than in the past, but overall, scholars assert that the scholarships of teaching and engagement might best match comprehensives' distinctive teaching-oriented and regional missions.

Keeping in mind the faculty scholarly learning at comprehensives, the following section discusses barriers that might impede faculty scholarly learning.

Barriers to Faculty Scholarly Learning at Comprehensives

With the challenges facing comprehensives, we would be remiss if we did not highlight barriers for comprehensive faculty scholarly learning. These barriers can be categorized around the following issues: workload challenges, mission confusion, and lack of resources.

Workload Challenges

The career of the comprehensive faculty member is characterized as one with heavy teaching and advising loads, coupled with high expectations for service to the region/local community and cultural norms of being "always available" or "having face time" for students and colleagues. Moreover, the influence of institutional striving (O'Meara, 2007) potentially increases comprehensive faculty members' workloads when they have to supplement their scholarship of teaching and/or engagement with traditional research because of uncertainties around promotion and tenure guidelines. In a study that analyzed different types of institutions through the conceptual lens of Coser's (1974) "greedy institution," Wright et al. (2004) determined that comprehensive universities were the greediest of institutions because of the significant demands placed on faculty to engage in high-quality research, teaching, advising, and service. As such, comprehensives have been described as wearing too many hats, being spread thin, and facing "hyperprofessionality" (Gornall & Salisbury, 2012, p. 150), a term that highlights how faculty members are asked to "giv[e] more" and "go . . . beyond and above in the professional context" (p. 150). Within the concept of hyperprofessionality, a tension exists between the voluntary, self-directed work created by faculty members' passions and commitments and a dysfunctional workload, which holds implicit expectations that academics are always willing and able to do more (Gonzales & Terosky, 2016).

Mission Confusion

The current literature emphasizes that comprehensive faculty not only face a heavy workload, but perhaps even more important, are often asked to do divergent and contradictory tasks (Gonzales & Terosky, 2016). Cruz, Ellern, Ford, Moss, and White (2013) argued that the missions of comprehensives are the least defined of all types of institutions and "falls somewhere between the research focus of research institutions and the teaching focus of liberal arts colleges" (p. 15). For example, a comprehensive faculty member might be directed to conduct more traditional research but then criticized when she spends less time on regional needs or in her campus-based office. These contradictions result in comprehensives being characterized as unclear in their mission or identity and "in a permanent state of adolescence" (in Henderson, 2011, p. 37; see also Bogue & Aper, 2000; Selingo, 2000). As such, it is not surprising that faculty employed at comprehensive colleges and universities report being less happy with their careers than faculty at other types of institutions (Henderson, 2011) and have high levels of emotional strain related to earning and maintaining legitimacy as a productive research scholar (Gonzales & Terosky, 2016).

Shifts in the missions of comprehensives, often a result of the tension between striving and calls for alternative forms of scholarship, plays out in promotion and tenure expectations for its faculty. Although some progress has been noted for institutionalizing Boyer's (1990) different forms of scholarship into reward systems, the scholarship of discovery continues to garner the greatest prestige and reward; the scholarships of teaching and engagement often do not count in tenure or advancement at many institutions (Braxton et al., 2002; Huber & Hutchings, 2005; O'Meara, 2005b; O'Meara & Rice, 2005; Walker, Baepler, & Cohen, 2008). "We face the paradox of promoting a[n] SoTL agenda," noted Walker et al., "in an atmosphere that does not yet fully reward SoTL activities" (2008, p. 183). A study by Braxton et al. (2006) found that although faculty members reported positive views of the scholarship of teaching, they agreed that they, and their institutional and departmental colleagues, value the scholarship of discovery more. Like the scholarship of teaching, the scholarship of engagement faces its own obstacles, including questions about its rigor (O'Meara, 2002), confusion about an agreed-upon definition (Cruz et al., 2013), and concerns about evaluating its products (Cruz et al., 2013; O'Meara, 2002).

Lack of Resources

Comprehensive faculty members are asked to maintain heavy workloads and engage in a variety of types of scholarship—particularly the scholarship of discovery—often within a context that has low levels of research-related resources, such as laboratory facilities, graduate or research assistants, or budgets for material (Henderson, 2011; Wolf-Wendel & Ward, 2006), as well as a lack of an incentivizing reward structure (Henderson, 2011; Wolf-Wendel & Ward, 2006). Henderson (2011) noted, "faculty members at . . . state comprehensive universities are less likely to work in a setting with a rich research culture where the values and norms of research are apparent" (p. 39). Thus, comprehensive faculty report feeling overextended and underresourced to meet the requirements and expectations of their careers. In their study of state comprehensive university women faculty, Wolf-Wendel and Ward (2006) highlighted how this issue affected one of their participants: "I left the publish or perish rat race of graduate school" [only to find myself at a campus] "just like my graduate institution minus the resources" (p. 13). Although institutions engender the culture of striving, comprehensives often do not provide the infrastructure or time needed to foster scholarly productivity.

Opportunities for Faculty Scholarly Learning at Comprehensives

The current literature on faculty highlights ways in which faculty scholarly learning can best be supported at comprehensive colleges and universities. Recommended supports include broadening views of scholarship for comprehensive faculty and developing an infrastructure of support.

Broadening Views of Scholarship for Comprehensive Faculty

In alignment with Boyer's recommendations more than 25 years ago, one way to support the scholarly learning of faculty is to broaden and reward different forms of scholarship, especially scholarship grounded in the disciplinary passions (personal fulfillment) of faculty and the public obligation (teaching and regional missions) of comprehensives (Boyer, 1990; see Terosky & Gonzales, 2016). By empowering faculty members to engage in scholarship that meets these two highly intertwined needs, there is the opportunity for faculty to meet promotion and tenure requirements, serve their students' and community needs, and feel professionally and personally fulfilled. But the key is in allowing faculty members to determine which type or types of scholarship works and how they can best integrate their scholarly learning with their other career responsibilities.

Developing an Infrastructure of Support

In order to prioritize faculty scholarly learning at the institutional and individual level, there needs to be an infrastructure of support within comprehensive colleges and universities. At the institutional level, what supports are in place for faculty scholarly learning, such as in time (workload releases), materials, facilities, collaborative learning spaces (e.g., teaching commons, faculty learning communities, learning academies), professional development, and/or seed grants that promote knowledge expansion and creation (Richlin & Cox 2004; Shulman, 2004a,b; Walker et al., 2008)? At the individual level, what strategies could faculty members apply so as to best structure their work around maximizing opportunities for learning and minimizing other tasks. In their study of hyperprofessionality, Gornall and Salisbury (2012) suggested work management strategies, such as email-free days or times, rules for email response time, and focused sessions for writing or studying, that help to contain distraction. Neumann et al. (2006) introduced the concept of "strategic responses" based on their participants "personal and self-directed meaning-making" and related actions that assisted them in crafting careers that could maintain scholarly learning amidst a "disordered" setting (p. 92). An example of a strategic response is to "integrat[e] all forms of intellectual work," rather than subdivide tasks by category or appointment type, so that comprehensive faculty members' research, teaching, and service responsibilities build on one another rather than compete for time and attention (Colbeck & Wharton-Michael, 2006, p. 18).

Conclusion and Implications

This chapter presented key insights into the scholarly learning of faculty members employed in comprehensive colleges and universities. First, mission-related concerns significantly affect comprehensive faculty and their scholarly learning, with scholars calling the scholarships of teaching and engagement as essential contributions. However, the effect of striving institutions or mission confusion, according to studies of comprehensive faculty perceptions on workload and status, encourages faculty at comprehensives to increase their productivity in the scholarship of discovery. Although whether or not comprehensive faculty are producing more traditional research, scholars acknowledge that traditional research is more highly valued than other forms of scholarship. Second, like Boyer, scholars emphasize that one size does not fit all in terms of scholarly learning among comprehensive faculty members, as seen in the range of scholarly activities pursued by comprehensive faculty members. As such, institutions of higher education need to support comprehensive faculty members' passions for their subject matter learning and work while also encouraging a connection to the mission of comprehensives. Third, scholarly learning requires time and resources. The current workloads and infrastructures at comprehensives could hamper the scholarly learning of its key players in the learning enterprise.

With this review in mind, what might be some implications for policy and practice at comprehensive universities? We offer two suggestions. First, we recommend that comprehensive universities, preferably at the institutional level but also at the college and department level, engage in a facilitated strategic plan in which all stakeholders provide input on the mission of the university, the college, and the department. This is an essential step in transparent communication of priorities around teaching, research, and service for administrators and faculty members. Through the strategic planning process, stakeholders can determine key directions of the institution, as well as recognize needed resources to bring the shared vision of the mission to fruition. Far too often, administrators and faculty are not fully aware of each other's perspectives and directives, often resulting in the two sets of stakeholders not being aligned. A strategic planning session, facilitated by a trained professional, would likely open up lines of communications around priorities, especially during a time of the striving institution phenomenon as well as concretely outline needed resources.

Second, we suggest that faculty members, through the support of professional development staff and administrators, engage in career planning (also referred to as career mapping) in which they reflect on the purpose of their multifaceted roles as faculty members and determine the direction of their future work priorities as well as identify needed resources and networks. Career planning, especially if conducted in conjunction with academic leaders, such as the department chair, would assist faculty members in better aligning their own passions and pursuits within their scholarly learning with the mission and needs of the comprehensive university and its students. In this way, faculty members at comprehensives might be better equipped to engage in forms of scholarly learning that fulfill what educational philosopher David Hansen (1995) refers to as a crossroads between "a form of public service," and "personal fulfillment" (p. xiii).

In the next chapter, the scholarly learning of faculty employed in LACs is discussed.

Liberal Arts Colleges

THE SCHOLARLY LEARNING of faculty members employed at LACs is the focus of this chapter. We provide details about the defining characteristics of LACs, offer a working definition of this institution type, and include a discussion of the roles and responsibilities of their full-time faculty members. Relying on Boyer's forms of scholarship, key themes are presented from the literature (2000 to present day). We conclude this chapter by exploring barriers and opportunities for faculty members' scholarly learning in LACs.

Defining Liberal Arts Colleges and Their Students and Faculty

Mission

Close student–faculty relationships, small class sizes, innovative pedagogies, residential living and learning communities, and the original model of U.S. higher education are just a few of the ways in which LACs have been characterized by the media and among those who are a product of or employed by this institution type. Miller and Skinner (2012) have described the U.S. LAC as one of the most successful educational enterprises and is one that is often modeled globally or imitated in other institutional settings (Chopp, Frost, & Weiss, 2013). Known for a broad-based curriculum that is rooted in the arts and sciences, LACs are credited with developing the first-year experience, fostering living-learning communities, and for envisioning and supporting undergraduate research, scholarship, and creative inquiry (Baker, Baldwin, & Makker, 2012).

Ferrall (2011) presented an apt description of LACs: "The thesis here is simple. Society needs well and broadly educated citizens. The more liberally educated citizens it has, the stronger it will be. … Liberal arts colleges, while not the only vehicles for producing liberally educated citizens, are among the best" (p. 16). Liberal arts colleges continue to hold a necessary place in the higher education landscape despite the rise of the research university model and other institution types to contribute to the diversity of U.S. higher education. Established as teaching-focused institutions that predominantly educate undergraduate students, LACs have continued to fulfill their institutional missions and serve as a model for undergraduate education. In the words of Thelin (2011), LACs are the "antidote" to the large and impersonal university (p. 296).

Today, the Carnegie classification system defines baccalaureate institutions as those where baccalaureate or higher degrees represent at least 50% of all degrees but where fewer than 50 master's degrees or 20 doctoral degrees were awarded in the previous year. Additionally, as noted by Carnegie, some institutions above the master's degree threshold are also included in this category. Both Baccalaureate Colleges: Arts & Sciences Focus and Baccalaureate Colleges: Diverse Fields are in this category, which includes 574 institutions (Carnegie Classification, 2015). For the purpose of this chapter, LACs are defined as:

> *4-year institutions whose defining features include an undergraduate teaching-focused mission, residential living and learning environments, small class sizes, low student-to-faculty ratios, and award more than half of their undergraduate degrees in the arts and sciences. Few, if any, graduate degrees are awarded.*

We stray from the Carnegie Classification definition in keeping with the work of Breneman (1990) and later Baker et al. (2012). In their efforts to replicate and update Breneman's findings, Baker and colleagues (2012) found that only 130 institutions, out of the 212 institutions included in Breneman's research, met the definition presented over 25 years earlier. The focus in this chapter is solely on Baccalaureate Colleges: Arts & Sciences institutions.

Students

According to the Carnegie Classification (2015), Baccalaureate Colleges: Arts & Sciences institutions enroll 460,036 students across the 271 schools included in this category. This total enrollment figure equates to 5.8% of total undergraduate enrollment across all institution types in the United States. The average enrollment on a per institution basis is 1,698. LACs enroll full-time traditional-aged college students (18–22 years old) who graduate in 4 years. Given the residential nature of LACs, few students live off campus or commute.

An important challenge or rather criticism of LACs is the lack of or limited racial/ethnic and economic diversity of students enrolled by this institution type. Liberal arts colleges enroll predominantly White student population rating low on the diversity index (e.g., low structural diversity/low numerical representation of students from different racial and ethnic groups) according to research by Umbach and Kuh (2006). Further, despite several recent financial aid programs/initiatives aimed at increasing interest and attendance of low-income students, this population of students continues to be underrepresented at LACs ("Disappointing Progress," 2009).

Faculty

Faculty members are instrumental to the LAC experience, as they develop, deliver, and assess the educational experiences in which students engage. Talk to an LAC graduate and he will talk to you about his relationships with faculty members. Talk to a faculty member who attended an LAC as an undergraduate, and she will tell you it was that experience and the relationships forged with faculty members that inspired that pursuit of the professoriate.

The work of Baker et al. (in press) notes that although faculty members in LACs may see teaching as their primary roles, and rightfully so, their roles have continued to evolve and expand, perhaps more so compared to any other institution type. This contradicts the assumptions made about faculty life in LACs—that you go to a LAC to "just teach." In his essay about

TABLE 3
FSSE Time Allocation, Hours per Week, in Liberal Arts Colleges

	LAC *Lower Division Courses*	LAC *Upper Division Courses*
Teaching	23.64	26.86
Advising	5.19	5.10
Research	7.04	8.13
Service	7.32	8.30
TOTALS	**43.19**	**48.39**

earning tenure in small colleges, Hughes (2014) notes that although teaching and mentoring dominate faculty time at LACs, scholarship expectations are on the rise. "Some colleges—especially those that are the most prestigious—have very high scholarly expectations, some of which would rival a lot of research universities" (para. 7).

Two recent studies of LAC faculty looked specifically at faculty time allocations. The first presented is FSSE supported and administered by Indiana University, as a complement to the National Survey of Student Engagement. The second study of the faculty experience in LACs discussed in this section is the work done by Baker et al. (in press), which was a longitudinal, mixed-methods study of the faculty experience in LACs involving the 13 member institutions of the Great Lakes Colleges Association (GLCA).

According to FSSE (Indiana University, 2016) results, LAC faculty members who teach lower division courses spend, on average, 24 hours per week engaging in teaching and related activities, 5 hours advising students, 7 hours engaging in scholarly efforts, and 7 hours engaging in campus and community service, totaling to 43 hours per week. Their faculty peers who teach upper division courses teach, on average, 27 hours a week, 5 hours advising students, 8 hours participating in scholarly efforts, and 8 hours engaging in service activities, totaling to 48 hours per week (see Table 3). As evidenced from these data, faculty members' allocation for *work only* related activities exceeds the traditional 40-hour work week.

In *Developing Faculty in Liberal Arts Colleges*, Baker et al. (in press) explored the faculty experience and trends in faculty development across career

TABLE 4
Hours on Task Across the GLCA

Hours on Task	Full Professor	Associate Professor	Assistant Professor	Nontenure Track
Teaching/Prep	31.98	32.58	35.92*	36.35*
Scholarship	8.18*	6.34	5.85	8.17*
Service	11.01*	10.08*	8.59	5.02
Personal	21.43	27.16*	26.48*	22.39
Total Hours/Week	72.60	76.16	76.86	71.93

stages, ranks, and appointment types in the GLCA (www.glca.org). Twelve of the 13 institutions are ranked by *U.S. News World Report* as a Top 100 Liberal Arts College. Their efforts through the longitudinal, mixed-methods study called the *Initiative for Faculty Development in Liberal Arts Colleges* (IFDLAC) viewed faculty development as the cultivation of relationships between, and the alignment of practices across, faculty members and administrators. As part of their research, Baker et al. (in press) and Baker, Pifer, and Lunsford (2016) collected data about the time allocation for faculty, by career stage and appointment type, to account for both professional responsibilities as well as personal responsibilities as a means of sharing a holistic picture of faculty life in LACs.

Table 4 summarizes the time on task (teaching, scholarship, service, and personal) for all ranks and appointment types. Teaching included actual time in the classroom, time preparing for class, grading, and supporting students enrolled in courses. Advising was also included under teaching. Scholarship included data collection, data analysis, writing, and dissemination efforts. Service included time spent in administrative roles (e.g., department chair), committee work, student recruitment, or attendance at college-sponsored community events. Finally, personal time included caregiving and home responsibilities and volunteerism. Nontenure-track faculty members and assistant professors spend the greatest amount of time on teaching, including course preparation and student advising. Full professors and nontenure-track faculty members spend the most time on scholarship. Full and associate professors spend the greatest time on service. Associate and assistant professors reported the greatest amount of personal responsibilities, namely child and parental care.

Data shared through the FSSE and IFDLAC studies debunk the myth that LAC faculty members focus *only* on teaching. In fact, Baker et al.'s (in press) research revealed that although effective teaching is required to earn promotion and tenure as well as promotion to full professorship, lack of scholarship at either stage will result in an unsuccessful bid for promotion and tenure. This was a consistent finding across the GLCA institutions. Such knowledge should inform how LACs understand and support scholarly learning.

Challenges

Questions of relevance, graduates' employability, and transferrable skill development continue to keep liberal arts education in question, despite the rise of other institution types seeking to recreate such an educational experience on their larger campuses by way of residential living and learning communities and supporting a college of liberal arts. Contributing to these challenges are assumptions made about faculty roles and responsibilities, that despite their educational pedigrees, the faculty members employed in LACs only teach and mentor students and are not true scholars in their respective fields (Baker et al., in press). This narrow view takes away from the many contributions of liberal arts faculty members and is not an accurate depiction of their professional activity and time allocations (Baker et al., in press; Indiana University, 2016).

Although LACs have been the focus of researchers of higher education for decades (see for example Nelson, 1981; Clark, 1987a, 1987b), it was the work of Breneman (1990) and his provocative question, "Are we losing our liberal arts colleges?" that shined a spotlight on this institution type and an alarming trend within this sector of higher education. At the time of his research, the Carnegie Classification identified 540 LACs; however, Breneman found that only 212 institutions from that list were true LACs in that they awarded at least half of their degrees in the arts and sciences; supported a residential living and learning experience; enrolled full-time students ranging in age from 18–22; and limited the number of majors to roughly 20 in the arts, humanities, languages, social sciences, and physical sciences. In his view, many of the "traditional" LACs that once existed, were in fact disappearing or morphing into what he describes as professional colleges. Years later, Morphew (2009) described this phenomenon as "academic drift," or "the tendency of colleges and universities to ape the programmatic offerings of the most prestigious [institutions]" and "as the gravest threat to institutional diversity" (p. 246). The notion of "academic drift" or "striving institutions" was first introduced in the fourth chapter of this monograph, as connected to comprehensive colleges and universities, given their lower status in the academic hierarchy (Morphew, 2002; O'Meara, 2007). LACs have not been immune to succumbing to academic drift as a means of survival and re-gaining relevance in U.S. higher education (Baker & Baldwin, 2015).

Summary

Since the publication of Breneman's (1990) study, the state of LACs continues to be pressworthy (e.g., Kiley, 2012a; Lane, 2013); however, the state of LACs may simply be a signal of a larger transitional period in higher education overall (Baker et al., 2012) experienced by and responded to differently by all institution types rather than a death knell for LACs, specifically. Using an evolutionary model as a lens to examine LACs, Baker and Baldwin (2015) concluded this sector of higher education was, in fact, going through a transitional period. In their efforts to maintain standing in the higher education landscape, LACs needed to adapt and respond to external and internal challenges in varying ways while also attempting to stay true to their liberal arts missions as a means of survival (Baker & Baldwin, 2015). Such adaptation requires a delicate balance, as LACs seek to appeal to today's students, respond to societal demands, and keep the liberal arts education ideals at the center of those responses.

Faculty Scholarly Learning in Liberal Arts Colleges

Liberal arts colleges are known for creating deep learning opportunities at the undergraduate student level (Baker et al., 2012). This type of deep learning requires students to not only understand their subject matter, but to have a mastery that allows them to apply that knowledge, and understand how it spans disciplines as critical to asking important questions within and across fields of inquiry. Assumptions are incorrectly made that similar learning experiences and approaches are applied to faculty members' professional and personal development, particularly in the ways in which academic work and faculty development are supported (Baker et al., in press). Very few studies of academic work or the faculty experience in LACs explicitly applies scholarly learning as a lens (an exception includes, Terosky & Gonzales, 2016). Further, little research about academic work in the context of LACs examines scholarly learning, explicitly or implicitly, across Boyer's four forms of scholarship (exceptions include Terosky & Gonzales, 2015, 2016; Baker et al., in press). Returning to Boyer's types of scholarship, the following section includes an overview of research that explores the faculty experience or academic work in LACs.

Scholarship of Discovery
The scholarship of discovery focuses on knowledge production and advancement through original research (Boyer, 1990). In LACs, the scholarship of discovery occurs by way of publications and disciplinary presentations. The work of Terosky and Gonzales (2016) is the only research to date to apply scholarly learning as a lens in LACs. Their findings revealed that faculty members engage in all four forms of scholarship, and they do so in thoughtful and compelling ways. Their faculty participants were heavily engaged in constructing new knowledge for discovery and published their work in scholarly peer-reviewed journals, as book chapters, and through laboratory experiments. Furthermore, collaborations with peers and students helped them engage in knowledge creation and dissemination activities and further enriched their development and engagement in knowledge for discovery.

Scholarship of Teaching
The dominant focus on the faculty experience in LACs relates to the scholarship of teaching, or the study of teaching and learning processes that involves public sharing, application, and evaluation by others (Boyer, 1990). Examples of the scholarship of teaching in a LAC environment might include a symposium on teaching and learning in which faculty members share strategies and lessons learned in the classroom or an internal blog site where faculty

members share short stories and pedagogical tools including an examination of the process of inquiry related to teaching and learning.

Literature about the scholarship of teaching in LACs focuses on research and practice (D'Avanzo, 2009; Holmgren, 2005; Mooney, Fordham, & Lehr, 2005; Ortquist-Ahrens, & Weispfenning, 2007; Peters, Schodt, & Walczak, 2008) in the context of centers for teaching and learning (CTLs). Two dominant streams of research are available: creating and sustaining CTLs and CTLs as facilitators of faculty development.

Researchers and practitioners have published work that provides a framework for creating space on campuses to discuss and support development in the areas of teaching and learning as well as best practices in sustaining and assessing such efforts and physical spaces (D'Avanzo, 2009; Pascarella, Cruce, Wolniak, & Blaich, 2004; Sorcinelli, 2002). D'Avanzo (2009) shared the story of Hampshire College and the creation of the campus center for teaching and learning. The goal of the center was to provide a space to identify areas of focus related to teaching and learning, to design and implement programming ideas, and to think creatively about how to evaluate such efforts. In addition to providing a case study of how to create a CTL in a LAC, an important contribution of this work was the discovery that cross-college conversation was abnormal on campus at the time the CTL was created and programming commenced, despite assumptions such conversations were prevalent given the size and mission of the institution. Such information allowed campus leaders and faculty developers to be more strategic in programming topic selection as a means of creating cross-campus discussions about teaching and learning as well as a deeper examination into the SoTL. This line of work serves an important function in ongoing conversations about academic work, particularly in support of scholarly learning in LACs. CTLs are also essential to their contribution to faculty development in the areas of teaching and learning.

Researchers and practitioners that have explored the connection between CTLs and faculty development (Keig, 2000; Lieberman, 2005) have highlighted the types of resources and support available to early career faculty members to support their transition into their new roles (Fayne & Ortquist-Ahrens, 2006); CTLs as a source for formal and informal support for faculty members across career stages (Chism, Lees, & Evenbeck, 2002; Sorcinelli,

2002); and as a means of promoting best practices in faculty development in LACs regionally and nationally (Persellin & Goodrick, 2012).

A prominent face and name in the study and practice of teaching and learning as connected to faculty development in liberal arts and other small colleges is Michael Reder, director of the Joy Shechtman Mankoff Center for Teaching & Learning at Connecticut College. Reder (2007) poses the question, "Does Your College *Really* Support Teaching and Learning?" In this essay, he argues that good teaching, given the mission of the LACs, is assumed to be happening naturally. "Not surprisingly, most administrators are complicit with the idea that good teaching always happens on their campuses, without the need for support or intervention" (p. 9). He further asserts, "Too many institutions are failing miserably when it comes to actually supporting faculty to become the most effective teachers possible" (p. 9). He argues that such a view creates the belief that CTL supports are about remediation to address poor teaching, rather than sources of renewal, innovation, and cross-disciplinary conversations about teaching and learning.

Efforts underway that align with the principles outlined by Reder, Mooney, Holmgren, and Kuerbis (2009) include those of the HBCU Faculty Development Network. Although not exclusively for LACs, this is a small network of 15 institutions committed to promoting effective teaching and student learning through collaborative activities and by way of faculty development supports of which can be accessed individually or through institutional membership. An aim of collaborative activities is to help connect teaching, research, and service more deliberately given the ways in which academic work is enacted. Network efforts also facilitate collaborations between faculty and administrators to be more thoughtful and all encompassing about achieving success to meet students' needs.

We make a cautionary note, however, about CTLs and the literature just discussed. Although CTLs work to offer practical implications to improve teaching practices, not all support or participate in efforts to engage in conducting scholarship related to teaching. Although the faculty development supports are critical to supporting faculty in LACs, that support does not always involve inquiry that is of a scholarly or research nature as described by Boyer (1990) in his characterization of the scholarship of teaching.

The work of Peters et al. (2008) draws attention to the assumption that SoTL would be a natural fit in LACs given the teaching-focused mission. However, their work revealed that few liberal arts institutions were actively engaged in national initiatives aimed at truly supporting the development of their faculties to engage in SoTL. At the time of their participation in the Carnegie Academy for the Scholarship of Teaching and Learning's (CASTL) program, only three LACs were among the 96 participating institutions at that time. They highlighted an alarming reason to explain this lack of LAC participation, which was traced to faculty rewards systems or rather the missing acknowledgment in evaluation criteria of the importance of this contribution. Through their participation and their own on-campus efforts, they offered a model to other liberal arts and small colleges to better support SoTL and to acknowledge the variety of ways in which scholarship could be enacted in LACs.

Scholarship of Engagement

The scholarship of engagement seeks to push beyond service duties to instead focus on rigor and the application of disciplinary expertise that can be shared and/or evaluated by peers (Boyer, 1990). The work of Heffner, Curry, and Beversluis (2006) examined engaged scholarship at Calvin College (a Christian LAC in Michigan) and the role it plays in the life of the college. Their research provided insights into faculty and student experiences related to service-learning and community-based teaching. Through this process of focusing on engaged scholarship more explicitly, the authors revealed that "faculty members began to see how community issues and strengths could not only shape learning goals and teaching activities but also transform scholarly questions and research methods" (Heffner et al., 2006, p. 120). Their research discussed the ways in which a focus on engagement also informed scholarship, teaching, and learning and supported more focused, related discourse on campus.

Scholarship of Integration

The scholarship of integration is characterized as the synthesis of information across disciplines, topics within a discipline, or time. Love (2008) highlighted a critical challenge in faculty work in LACs related to the scholarship of integration. Despite their efforts to support students' ability to think about and pursue learning in more intentionally connected ways, little or no supports (or space) are provided to help faculty members engage in similar learning experiences, and one would assume such opportunities would be provided to faculty members employed in LACs given the very deliberate connection between integration and student learning. As Love (2008) so aptly writes, "If integrative teaching and learning are to be authentic and sustainable, then faculty need to renew their sense of discovery and joy in making connections and to allow these feelings to shape the integrative opportunities they create for students" (p. 267). This quotation raises an important point about providing the skills, developmental opportunities, and space to faculty members as they hone their abilities in order to create learning opportunities for students and to guide them through their own journeys.

In summary, as authors, we were challenged to find research (or practice) that explores scholarly learning in LACs beyond the work of Baker et al. (in press) or Terosky and Gonzales (2016). Further, the majority of research about the faculty experience in LACs focuses on the scholarship of teaching, which we argue misrepresents academic work in a 21st century LAC and the variety of ways in which faculty members engage in and support their own learning. The following section highlights barriers to faculty scholarly learning in LACs.

Barriers to Faculty Scholarly Learning in Liberal Arts Colleges

Our section on scholarly learning in LACs was limited beyond a discussion of the scholarship of teaching. This disproportionate review, unfortunately, is an accurate accounting of available research and practice, which examines or portrays academic work, the faculty experience, or faculty development in LACs. Such a reality highlights three barriers to faculty scholarly learning in LACS: inaccurate assumptions about academic work, inadequate faculty development supports, and disconnections between expectations and reward/incentive structures.

Inaccurate Assumptions About Academic Work in LACs

Based on the literature shared in this chapter it is clear that assumptions are made about how, and in what ways, faculty members engage in academic work. Very few studies or case studies of the faculty experience or academic work explore Boyer's conceptualization of the scholarship of integration, engagement, or discovery in LACs. Those assumptions situate LAC faculty members squarely, and almost exclusively, in the scholarship of teaching thus failing to account for the realities of this evolving institution type and the demands on faculty members' time. FSSE data and the work of Baker et al. (in press) provide evidence that LAC faculty members do engage in other areas of faculty work beyond teaching and learning to highlight the growing role of scholarship, engagement, and integration.

Scholarship is an important aspect of faculty life in LACs. Although faculty members in LACs are not expected to have the same quantity of publications as their research university peers, they are expected to publish high-quality, peer-reviewed works and be actively engaged in their scholarly and professional conferences and associations. For example, in the career advice section of Inside Higher Ed, an essay published in 2015 titled, *A Guide for Applying to Jobs at Selective Liberal Arts Colleges*, includes seven tips for preparing to interview at a selective LAC. Number one on that list was the advice that "research matters" (para. 2). Accompanying this tip was a discussion on the importance of a robust research program as evidenced by regularly scholarly conference attendance and presentations as well as published articles and chapters by reputable publishers: "While the research requirements at SLACs (selective liberal arts colleges) are less intense than at top research universities, at the same time, there is the expectation (and support for) scholars to be highly engaged with their research program, to have their teaching informed by their research program, and to be engaged with other experts in their field" (para. 2). The essay also notes the importance of teaching, curriculum, interactions with students, and contributions to departmental, campus, and community activities. LAC faculty members do actively engage in all areas of faculty life, and institutional expectations are increasing across all domains of academic work, but faculty supports are not keeping up with those rising expectations (Baker et al., in press).

Inadequate Faculty Development Supports

Inaccurate assumptions about academic work in LACs lead to fewer resources to support faculty members as they engage in the variety of roles and responsibilities expected to support the mission of their institutions beyond that of teaching and learning. As a result, faculty members do not receive the needed supports to engage in other forms of scholarship as defined by Boyer. Baker and colleagues (in press) recommend conducting an assessment of faculty development supports to identify (a) who (or what) has responsibility for supporting faculty as they engage in academic work, (b) available faculty development supports to determine which populations are served by those programs, and (c) the intended (and achieved) outcomes of those programs. Such an assessment lays the groundwork for identifying redundancies, opportunities for growth, and supports the development and an assessment of a diversified faculty development portfolio that spans career stage and appointment type.

Disconnection Between Expectations and Reward/Incentive Structures

Inaccurate assumptions about academic work and inadequate faculty development support in LACs can be traced to institutional reward and incentive structures. Such disconnections are not unique or limited to LACs but are problematic given the evolution underway and the rising expectations on faculty members' time in this institution type (Baker & Baldwin, 2015; Baker et al., in press; Peters, Schodt, & Walczak, 2008).

As part of their research through the IFDLAC, Baker, Pifer, and Lunsford (2016) reviewed faculty handbooks and evaluation criteria and interviewed faculty members who had or currently held positions on their institutional personnel committees. Disconnections between policy as outlined in the faculty handbook and actual practice (e.g., interim reviews and tenure decisions) were on the rise and created challenges for committee members when evaluating pretenure faculty members and for those aspiring for promotion to full professorship. Further, Baker and colleagues' review of written handbook language was mismatched to what they heard from faculty members and administrators as to what is expected and valued on their respective campuses. Although scholarship, for example, was included as important in all 13 GLCA faculty handbooks/evaluation criteria, there was no clear direction as to how scholarship was defined, supported, and evaluated (Baker et al., in press). Additionally, faculty handbook and evaluation criteria language did not wholly recognize all of Boyer's forms of scholarship, which neglects the realities of faculty life in LACs.

Opportunities for Scholarly Learning in Liberal Arts Colleges

Despite the barriers to scholarly learning discussed in this chapter, administrators, faculty developers, and faculty members have a great deal of opportunity to support scholarly learning for their faculties. LACs serve as incubators for student development and experiential learning opportunities modeled by other institution types (Baker et al., 2012). LACs can also serve as developers of supports and processes to aid faculty scholarly learning. Those opportunities include redefining faculty learning more broadly, modernizing existing faculty development supports, and aligning policy and practice.

Redefining Faculty Learning in LACs

Much like learning at the student level is broadly defined and supported across disciplines and experiences (Kreber, 2009), so too can it be broadly defined and supported by the faculty members employed in LACs. As noted earlier, we are aware of only one study of the faculty experience in LACs that explicitly relied on scholarly learning as a theoretical lens (Terosky & Gonzales, 2016).

An important finding from the work of Terosky and Gonzales (2016) is the realization that by engaging in all four forms of scholarship, the faculty members who participated in the study also found personal fulfillment through a continued, and deep engagement in disciplinary work. Participants discussed their sense of fulfillment in applying that knowledge to a greater good, while also using these opportunities as a means of infusing some vitality into their careers, particularly for mid-career faculty members.

Modernizing Faculty Development Supports

Knowledge from Terosky and Gonzales (2016), Baker et al. (in press), and Indiana University (2016) revealed that faculty members do engage in scholarship broadly defined beyond teaching and learning. Such a reality aligns with faculty life in a 21st-century LAC and the myriad ways in which faculty members engage in academic work. Relying on this knowledge, administrators, faculty developers, and faculty members have an opportunity to reenvision faculty development supports. Terosky and Gonzales (2016) findings confirmed how, and in what ways, faculty scholarly learning is occurring in LACs, thus facilitating the development of institutional supports that further develop and encourage faculty members' engagement in scholarship broadly defined. Baker et al. (in press) revealed the importance of career stage, appointment type, and disciplinary/divisional realities as important factors that must be accounted for when seeking to develop, implement, and assess a more strategic, well-rounded faculty development portfolio. When faculty development supports are perceived as valueless, participation is low, which is demoralizing for faculty members as well as the administrators and faculty developers charged with creating such supports.

Aligning Policy and Practice

As the professoriate changes, so do the ways in which policy and practice are enacted and recorded. Returning to the faculty development portfolio assessment discussed (Baker et al., in press), such an assessment supports a formal comparison between current practice and programming as stated in evaluation criteria and other relevant information in faculty handbook language. A comparison of this kind allows for an examination of how, and in what ways, current policy and practice are aligned or misaligned and further supports the identification of needed development supports by faculty members. The faculty handbook is perhaps the most important document in that it communicates what is and is not valued in a given institution. Faculty roles and responsibilities are highlighted—if administrators and faculty developers expect faculty members to be proficient in the areas noted, programming to support development in those areas must be accounted for as part of a diversified and strategic faculty development portfolio.

Conclusion and Implications

Because the LAC is known as a test kitchen for curricular innovations in undergraduate education (Baldwin & Baker, 2009), LAC faculty members expectedly spend the majority of their time engaged in the SoTL as aligned with their institutional missions. However, as evidenced in recent research about the LAC faculty experience (Baker et al., in press; Terosky & Gonzales, 2016), LAC faculty members engage in scholarly learning across all of Boyer's (1990) forms of scholarship. As such, we envision opportunities for administrators and faculty members to support the scholarly learning of their faculties.

We suggest the need to broaden views about the faculty experience in LACs along with providing corresponding supports and aligning reward and incentive structures as paramount to providing a realistic account of the faculty experience and academic work in the 21st-century LAC. A study participant in the research by Baker and colleagues (in press) noted that the focus on teaching, as connected to institutional mission, underestimates and miscommunicates the importance of engaging in the scholarship of discovery and other areas of faculty life, particularly as it relates to promotion and tenure. As noted previously, administrators and faculty members need to review handbook and evaluation criteria language to make sure policy and practice are aligned and that incoming faculty members are given a realistic job preview of faculty life. Such efforts ensure that corresponding expectations are accurate and consistent. We note that a revision to policy does not discount the importance of teaching in this institutional setting but rather accurately reflects current expectations and the evolving nature of roles and responsibilities in LACs. Such changes also reflect Boyer's forms of scholarship and thus provide more clear connections between the myriad ways in which LAC faculty are currently engaging and concrete ways in which to support and acknowledge that learning in all areas of academic life in LACs. We also believe such reenvisioning may be a means of not only maintaining relevance in U.S. higher education but also providing an opportunity for LACs to serve as exemplars in faculty scholarly learning of which other institution types seek to model.

We explore the scholarly learning of community college faculty in the next chapter.

Community Colleges

SCHOLARLY LEARNING OF community college faculty is the focus of this chapter. We begin by defining community colleges and providing background information on their history, missions, and students. Next, a profile of the community college professoriate is included followed by a depiction of their work and work contexts. Then, we discuss studies regarding scholarly learning of faculty members at this institutional type. This chapter concludes by exploring barriers and opportunities for scholarly learning at community colleges.

Defining Community Colleges and Their Students and Faculty

Founded in 1901 as an extension of secondary schools, 2-year colleges play an instrumental role in delivering U.S. higher education. In the 2014–2015 academic year, 2-year colleges constituted 35% of all U.S. postsecondary institutions (Carnegie Classification of Institutions of Higher Education, 2015). Among the 1,616 two-year colleges reported, 920 were publically controlled, whereas 696 were privately controlled (Snyder, de Brey, & Dillow, 2016b, Table 317.10). Of the privately controlled 2-year colleges, 608 were for profit, and 88 were nonprofit (Snyder et al., Table 317.10). The earliest term applied to 2-year colleges was junior colleges. Today, 2-year colleges are interchangeably and variably referred to as community colleges, city colleges, county colleges, and technical colleges, among other names. The terms employed are typically associated with the individual institution's focus and/or sponsor (Cohen, Brawer, & Kisker, 2014). For consistency purposes, in this chapter, we refer to this institutional type as a community college defined as *a regionally accredited public or private nonprofit institution of higher education at which the highest degree awarded is generally the associate in arts or the associate in science.*

Mission

As maintained by Meier (2013) and supported by additional scholars, "there is a history of ambiguity, even confusion, regarding the mission and purposes of the [community] colleges" (p. 3). In broadest terms, as described by the American Association of Community Colleges (AACC, n.d.), "the mission of the community college is to provide education for individuals, many of whom are adults, in its service region" (para. 1). Vaughan (2006) framed the community college mission as a series of commitments that included "serving all segments of society through an open-access admissions policy that offers equal and fair treatment to all students, comprehensive educational program, serving its community as a community-based institution of higher education, teaching,; and lifelong learning" (p. 3). These commitments are often advanced through multiple curricular functions (Cohen et al., 2014).

In the sixth edition of *The American Community College,* Cohen et al. (2014) identified the following interrelated functions: (a) academic transfer education, (b) occupational education, (c) continuing education, (d) developmental education, and (e) community service. Nevertheless, each community college has its own mission and may emphasize one function over another (AACC, n.d.; Cohen et al., 2014; Vaughan, 2006). Furthermore, in some cases, institutions are differentiated by historical commitments to serve a particular population, such as HBCUs, and as an emerging phenomenon, as minority-serving institutions[1] serving and being funded in specific (though limited ways) to serve particular ethnic/cultural groups that have historically been disadvantaged (Conrad & Gasman, 2015; Gasman, Baez, & Turner, 2008).

---

[1] MSIs include Historically Black Colleges and Universities (HBCUs), Tribal Colleges and Universities (TCUs), Hispanic Serving Institutions (HSIs), and Asian American and Native American Pacific Islander Serving Institutions (AANAPISIs).

Moreover, although the highest degree awarded by the community college has been the associate in arts or the associate in science (Cohen et al., 2014), an increasing number of states have authorized community colleges to confer their own baccalaureate degrees (Cohen et al., 2014; Levin, 2004; Russell, 2010; Walker, 2005). This trend has markedly contributed to the complexity of the community college mission and identity (Floyd, 2005; Levin, 2004). In fact, as suggested by Floyd (2005), "what we find in the field is the emergence of a new institutional type that embodies characteristics of different existing institutional types" (p. 37).

Students

Often referred to as the people's college, democracy's college, or the open-door college (Cohen et al., 2014), the community college serves as a primary access point to higher education for various student populations and in particular underrepresented minorities. In fall 2014, community colleges enrolled 45% of all U.S. undergraduates and 41% of all first-time freshmen (AACC, 2016). During the same time, 57%, 52%, and 62% of all Latino, Black, and Native American students respectively enrolled in higher education attended a community college (AACC, 2016). Furthermore, 57% of community college students were women, 36% of all students were the first in their families to attend college, 7% were non-U.S. citizens, and 4% were veterans (AACC, 2016). As suggested by Malcolm (2013), "the factors that lead diverse groups of students to enroll in community colleges are both complex and nuanced" (p. 19).

Faculty

National goals such as increasing the number of college graduates and producing a globally competitive workforce have propelled community colleges and their students to the fore of public discussion (White House, 2010, 2014). However, faculty within this sector of higher education have not received the public, professional, and scholarly attention they deserve (Braxton, 2015; Townsend & Twombly, 2007; Twombly & Townsend, 2008). Similar to faculty at comprehensive universities (Gardner, 2013), community college faculty members are significantly understudied. Indeed, scholars have aimed to address the scarcity of literature focused on community college faculty work, careers, and experiences (Braxton, 2015; Levin, Kater, & Wagoner, 2006; Outcalt, 2002; Townsend & Twombly, 2007).

Still there remains a gap in our understanding of the community college professoriate. Although the complicated origins and missions of the community college are recognized in the literature (Ayers, 2005; Cohen et al., 2014; Levin, 2000, 2004; Vaughan, 2006), the work of its faculty is often oversimplified (Gonzales & Ayers, in press). Experts note that limited knowledge about community college faculty, unfair comparisons, and consistent application of frameworks more suitable for studying faculty at 4-year institutions has engendered assumptions regarding their contributions to the field of higher education, their students, and their respective disciplines (Gonzales & Ayers, in press; Townsend & Twombly, 2007; Twombly & Townsend, 2008). In the words of Townsend and Twombly (2007), "community college faculty are ignored in the literature about faculty, and at worst, the literature perpetuates negative stereotypes about them" (p. 3).

Although what is known about community college faculty is limited, we know that they make up nearly 25% of all faculty in degree-granting postsecondary institutions (Snyder et al., 2016a, Table 315.10). Moreover, most community college faculty are employed on a contingent basis. Contingent generally refers to both part-time and full-time nontenure-track faculty; nonetheless, in the community college most appointments are part time. The most recent data show that in fall 2013, 70% of community college faculty held part-time appointments (Snyder et al., 2016a Table 313.30).

The majority of community college faculty members are also women (Schuster & Finkelstein, 2006), White (Townsend & Twombly, 2007), and likely to hold a bachelor's or master's degree (Cohen et al., 2014; Schuster & Finkelstein, 2006). In 2003–2004, 55% of community college faculty reported a master's degree as the highest degree earned (Cataldi, Fahimi, Bradburn, & Zimbler, 2005); Provasnik & Planty, 2008). That same year, 12% of public community college faculty and 20% of private community college faculty reported a doctorate as the highest degree earned (Cataldi, Fahimi, Bradburn, & Zimbler, 2005)Provasnik & Planty, 2008). Unsurprisingly, part-time faculty held fewer advanced degrees. As reported by Eagan (2007), 8.6%

of part-time faculty and 17.9% of full-time faculty teaching at community colleges in 2004 held a doctoral degree. Although doctorate degree holders have been historically frowned upon by the community college, given their training and socialization as researchers and not teachers (Cohen et al., 2014; Kozeracki, 2002), the percentage of community college faculty with doctorates continues to increase. Most recently, Braxton (2015) reported that 19% of community college faculty have a doctoral degree. The increase in faculty with doctorates at the community college has been associated with the increasingly competitive job market (Austin, 2002; Jenkins, 2012; Schuster & Finkelstein, 2006) as well as the increase in baccalaureate degree-granting community colleges (Jenkins, 2012).

Community college faculty are also likely to be working in unionized environments (Cohen et al., 2014; Levin et al., 2006). Based on data from the National Center for the Study of Collective Bargaining in Higher Education and the Professions, Cohen et al. (2014) noted that in 2011, 43% of full-time and 28% of part-time faculty in public community colleges were working under collective bargaining agreements, which inevitably shape elements of faculty work (Levin et al., 2006; Rhoades, 1998; Wolf-Wendel, Ward, & Twombly, 2007).

Faculty responsibilities align with the teaching mission of the community college. As explained by Townsend and Twombly (2007) "given the community college's overarching mission of providing open access to higher education, the most important role of community college faculty members is to teach, and they do teach" (p. 37). Using data from the 2004 National Study of Postsecondary Faculty (NSOPF), Provasnik and Planty (2008) reported that 89% of community college faculty indicated teaching as their main activity. Faculty service is also central to the community college mission. Service takes many forms. Broadly speaking, faculty may engage in institutional, disciplinary, community, and scholarly service (O'Meara et al., 2008); however, community college faculty service is usually limited to institutional and community service (Cohen et al., 2014; Fugate & Amey, 2000; Townsend & Twombly, 2007).

Whereas 89% of community college faculty identified teaching as their main activity, 3% indicated administration, 8% noted other activities, and

0.1% cited research as their main activity (Provasnik & Planty, 2008). Accordingly, scholars such as Hagedorn (2015) note, "community college faculty research could be considered an oxymoron" (p. 49). Similarly, Cohen et al. (2014) suggest, "no one speaks of the community college professor's research load, scholarship load, or consulting load" (p. 89). Nonetheless, it is necessary to note that given traditional and narrow views and definitions of research/scholarship, faculty may not label their efforts as research (Cejda & Hensel, 2009; Tinberg, Duffy, & Mino, 2007).

Challenges

U.S. community colleges and campus leaders face major challenges such as upholding the multiple missions of the community college (Eddy, 2012; Wood & Nevarez, 2014), responding to the nation's developmental education crisis (Acevedo-Gil, Santos, & Solorzano, 2014; Bailey, 2009), and addressing low completion and transfer rates (Bailey, Jaggars, & Jenkins, 2015). Although lauded for serving students who have been historically marginalized and placed at greater risk for not completing college, the community college has been criticized for low transfer and completion rates. Overall, only 14% of students starting in community colleges transfer and earn a baccalaureate within 6 years. Similarly, only 32% earn a certificate or associate's degree within 6 years (Jenkins & Fink, 2016). However, critics often fail to acknowledge the numerous factors contributing to such figures, such as limited institutional resources, academic and financial barriers, and conflicting obligations (Cohen et al., 2014; Levin, 2007).

Contending with dwindling, insufficient, and shifting revenue streams (Cohen et al., 2014; Goldrick-Rab, 2010; Nevarez & Wood, 2010) and operating within a culture of increased audit and accountability (Eddy, 2010, 2012) are additional challenges facing community colleges. Furthermore, as previously noted an increasing number of community colleges are now offering and conferring baccalaureate degrees (Martinez, 2014; McKinney, Scicchitano, & Johns, 2013), which challenges institutional identity (Levin, 2004). To date, 22 states have authorized community colleges to award baccalaureate degrees (Gandara & Cuellar, 2016). Although Walker (2005) emphasized the difficulty in identifying the first instance of this trend, Russell

(2010) suggested that West Virginia approved the first program in 1989. Justifications for this development are primarily grounded in notions of access (McKinney et al., 2013), efforts to meet state workforce needs (Walker, 2005), increased credential requirements for various professions (Bemmel, Floyd, & Bryan, 2008), limited enrollment capacities at 4-year colleges (Russell, 2010), and a desire for increased prestige on behalf of the community colleges (Dougherty & Townsend, 2006; Toma, 2012). Whereas some contend that the community college baccalaureate is a form of mission creep, or broadened focus beyond originally set goals and functions (Fain, 2013; Longanecker, 2008; Toma, 2012), others maintain that by offering baccalaureate degrees, the community college fulfills its institutional commitments (Walker, 2005). As Walker (2005) explained, the community college baccalaureate is viewed as a "natural progression" (p. 16) of the community college mission to meet student and community needs. Regardless, this trend is expected to continue to expand to other states.

Summary

In sum, community colleges are multifaceted organizations that face numerous challenges. In all their complexity, they play a crucial role in the U.S. higher education system, particularly in terms of expanding access to higher education for historically underrepresented students. Understanding the community college context is central to the examination of community college faculty scholarly learning, which we turn to next.

Faculty Scholarly Learning at Community Colleges

As previously noted, community college faculty have received limited scholarly attention. We know little about their work lives. With the exception of a few studies, we know even less about their scholarly learning. Therefore, in addition to community college and higher education literature, we relied on some discipline-specific literature to help explore this topic. Most studies, however, did not explicitly apply scholarly learning as a theoretical lens in order to study faculty work. In fact, Terosky and Gonzales's (2016) work is the only scholarship to apply this lens. We also drew heavily from a recent special issue of *New Directions for Community Colleges* edited by Braxton (2015), which seeks to address the question: "To what extent are community college faculty members engaged in research and scholarship?" (p. 1). To help address this overarching research question, Braxton and colleagues employed Boyer's (1990) lens, which was also used to help conceptualize scholarly learning in this monograph. In the following section, we present a broad overview of how faculty support their scholarly learning. Then, we delve deeper into how scholarly learning, per Boyer's framework, plays out in the community college context.

Scholarship of Discovery

Cohen and Brawer (1977) once noted that community college faculty "care for students, not research; for information transmission, not knowledge generation" (p. 46). Although faculty continue to care for students (Cohen et al., 2014; McArthur, 2005) their lack of interest and disengagement in research/scholarship has been debunked. In fact, an increasing number of studies highlight faculty members advancing both applied research and traditional/basic research agendas, often in collaboration with their students (Cejda & Hensel, 2009; Perez, 2003; Martinez, 2012, 2014; Terosky & Gonzales, 2016). These collaborations are generally framed and discussed as undergraduate research. To date, an increasing number of organizations, such as the Council on Undergraduate Research (CUR), Community College Undergraduate Research Initiative (CCURI), National Council of Instructional Administrators (NCIA), and Beacon Conference, are facilitating and supporting undergraduate research at the community college. For example, in collaboration with the CUR and NCIA, Hensel and Cejda (2015), worked with 104 community colleges and more than 400 faculty members to develop action plans for the implementation of undergraduate research programs on their campuses "beyond a few committed professors" (para. 9).

Prior to this work, Cejda and Hensel (2009) identified four categories of undergraduate research in community colleges: (a) incorporating research into the curriculum, (b) using research activities in place of 'cookbook' laboratories or assignments, (c) conducting applied research at the community college, and (d) conducting basic research at the community college (http://www.cur.org/urcc/ch1-03/). These categories clearly intersect with the four domains of scholarship outlined by Boyer (1990). One example of undergraduate research is the work on diabetes and other Navajo health problems by students and faculty at Diné College (Ambler, 1999; "Diné College," 2001), the first tribally controlled community college in the United States. According to Ambler (1999) "for more than 25 years, the college has taken a lead role in researching Navajo health problems, utilizing students to help conduct research" (para. 3). The students' cultural connection and the college's commitment to the community have helped advance this work. Given the focus of this particular project, this work is mostly reflective of the scholarship of engagement/application.

However, the work of Terosky and Gonzales (2016) and Martinez (2012, 2014) highlights faculty collaborating with colleagues and students on traditional/basic research. Although usually undergraduate research at community colleges is led by one individual or a small group of interested faculty (Cejda & Hensel, 2009; Hensel & Cejda, 2015), two recent studies by Martinez (2012, 2014) highlight undergraduate research as an *expectation* for faculty teaching within baccalaureate degree programs. For example, in the first study (Martinez, 2012), one administrator described a conversation with a new faculty hire as follows:

> *I told them that your responsibilities would be teaching in a quality [said] program, one in which you will help to develop and be able to put your personal mark on, that includes research with undergraduates, as well as teaching, developing the new courses that are needed for the program, and maintaining, seeking research dollars to maintain a research agenda. (p. 11)*

Counter to commonly held assumptions, the studies presented here illustrate that community college faculty engage in the scholarship of discovery. This form of learning is achieved in collaboration with both colleagues and students, particularly through undergraduate research.

Scholarship of Teaching

The rich diversity of community college students calls for diverse approaches to teaching and learning. To engage diverse learners, community college faculty are strongly encouraged to focus on improving their pedagogical and curricular practices (Murray, 2002; Padovan & Whittington, 1998). "At a minimum it would appear that most if not all community college faculty members participate in the scholarship of teaching" (Townsend & Twombly, 2007, p. 39). The scholarship of teaching, defined as researching and applying pedagogical methods and sharing findings with colleagues, is typically supported at the organizational level through inservice training and professional development opportunities (Murray, 2002; Sperling, 2003; Townsend & Twombly, 2007). Murray's (2000, 2001, 2002) extensive work on faculty development in community colleges has identified multiple common organizational practices including: financial support for faculty to attend conferences, grants and release time to support innovation in teaching, teaching resource centers, workshops facilitated by outside experts, and possibly sabbatical leaves, among other activities. However, few faculties take advantage of the aforementioned resources, and we know little about their effectiveness, in part because of a lack of clear objectives (Murray, 2002). External support and collaborations centered on the scholarship of teaching have also been documented (Duffy, 2006).

Terosky and Gonzales (2016) provided clear examples of community college faculty engaged in the scholarship of teaching. Linda, a full professor of humanities at a community college who attended a disciplinary conference, shared an insight that reflects the scholarship of teaching:

> *I started to notice when I went to some of the presentations, the people whose presentations I loved the most. . . . were conducting classroom research. . . . so these presenters had done some research within their classrooms and had some pretty solid facts and figures to back up their methods. And that sort of excited me. So I came back, I thought, "Oh, I'm going to start some research and actually [start a classroom research group]." (p. 111)*

Just as Linda was inspired or motivated to start a classroom research group, in a recent study, Hagedorn (2015) demonstrated how the *Achieving the Dream: Community Colleges Count* initiative has inspired community college faculty to engage in scholarship to "improve their classrooms *and* promote sustainable student success" (p. 49). This process was illustrated through three vignettes developed from faculty interviews. Vignettes were centered on Temple College (TC), Macomb Community College (MCC), and Community College of Baltimore County (CCBC). Faculty engaged in various forms of learning. In addition to collecting and analyzing data, faculty developed interventions at TC, designed a new course at MCC, and created a new accelerated learning program at CCBC. In addition to supporting faculty research, participation in *Achieving the Dream* underscored the importance of data-driven decision-making. In sum, *Achieving the Dream* helped advance a culture of research and evidence at the colleges highlighted in this study (Hagedorn, 2015).

Although Terosky and Gonzales (2016) and Hagedorn (2015) noted elements that motivated faculty to engage in the scholarship of teaching, Sperling's (2003) work highlighted that community college faculty actually researched the concept of motivation. Faculty were interested in understanding motivation to inform their teaching practices. They explored questions such as: "What do we know about motivation? Why do some people want to learn and others don't? What sustains motivation? What hinders it? What practices promote high motivation over time?" (p. 597). This work allowed faculty to reflect on their teaching strategies and adopt new theoretically grounded pedagogical practices to engage students and enhance their learning. In sum, the scholarship of teaching is encouraged and occurring at community colleges. Faculty value teaching; nonetheless, not all capitalize on the various organizational efforts and supports available around teaching.

Scholarship of Engagement

The scholarship of engagement/application, along with the scholarship of teaching, has been identified as befitting community college faculty (Boyer, 1990; Braxton & Lyken-Segosebe, 2015). Scholarly learning reflective of the scholarship of application was observed in Terosky and Gonzales's (2016) work. In fact, of the participants engaged in the construction of knowledge, nearly half engaged in the scholarship of application. As suggested by Terosky and Gonzales (2016), this "speaks to the public good orientation of community and broad access liberal arts colleges" (p. 113). Specific activities that participants engaged in included writing letters to the editor and state policymakers regarding the marketization of higher education, developing a journal aimed at enlightening educators on this very topic, and participating in public art commissions.

Perniciaro, Nespoli, and Anbarasan's (2015) work also illustrates faculty immersion in the scholarship of engagement. Perniciaro et al. (2015) described a consortium of community colleges in New Jersey that was created to develop workforce training programs to meet the needs of local businesses. The goal of the consortium was to help address prevalent statewide issues such as unemployment, lack of employment growth, and limited employment opportunities for graduates, among other issues. Community college faculty members in New Jersey are engaged in helping address these issues through applied research, such as by assessing labor needs, outlining job demands, developing curriculum, and helping to secure competitive grants. Specifically related to the Center for Regional and Business Center at Atlantic Cape Community College, faculty also lent their expertise related to geographic information systems (GIS) mapping, social media, and health care. In sum, the studies discussed in this section highlight that community college faculty participate in the scholarship of engagement. In alignment with the community college mission, faculty use their knowledge and skills to address the needs of the community.

Scholarship of Integration

Although Terosky and Gonzales's (2016) study did not produce data that spoke of faculty scholarly learning associated with the scholarship of integration, Braxton and Lyken-Segosebe (2015) found that 43.7% of community college faculty have published one to two times within the past 5 years work that aligns with the scholarship of integration. Examples of publications highlighted by Braxton and Lyken-Segosebe (2015) included a literature review on disciplinary topic and a review essay of two or more books on similar topics (p. 10). Despite the high percentage of community college faculty Braxton and Lyken-Seogesbe (2015) found to be engaged in the scholarship of integration, the literature related to this domain is scarce. In sum, few scholars have examined the scholarly learning of faculty members as they engage in the scholarship of integration.

Summary of Faculty Scholarly Learning in Community Colleges
Although the scholarship of teaching and the scholarship of engagement/application are most befitting community college faculty (Boyer, 1990; Braxton & Lyken-Segosebe, 2015), the literature discussed in this chapter highlighted that community college faculty are engaged in all four domains, albeit to dissimilar degrees. Drawing from a sample of 2,352 tenured, tenure-track, and nontenure-track faculty in four academic disciplines (biology, chemistry, history, and sociology) across 200 community colleges, Park, Braxton, and Lyken-Segosebe (2015) identified three types of community college scholars: Immersed Scholars, Scholars of Pedagogical Practice, and Scholars of Dissemination. Immersed Scholars constituted 31% of the sample and were engaged in all four of Boyer's domains. Scholars of Pedagogical Practice, who made up 22% of the sample, were mostly engaged in Boyer's scholarship of teaching, and Scholars of Dissemination, encompassing 47% of the sample, blended the scholarships of integration and teaching.

Taken together, community college faculty are engaged in various scholarly learning activities. Nonetheless, the research presented in this chapter also shed light on contextual realities and barriers that limit faculty scholarly learning. To this point, we discuss both barriers and opportunities to scholarly learning at community colleges next.

Barriers to Faculty Scholarly Learning at Community Colleges

Community colleges are complex institutions in which to be situated— particularly for faculty. The complexity of these institutions influences the types and degree of scholarly learning that takes place. Although it is evident that scholarly learning is encouraged and supported at the community college, barriers to faculty scholarly learning are prevalent. These barriers can be sorted into the following categories: (a) heavy teaching loads, (b) narrow views of scholarship, and (b) limited resources and infrastructures.

Heavy Teaching Loads

The community college is a teaching institution. Therefore, it is no surprise that faculty devote or allocate most of their time to teaching. As previously noted, 89% of community college faculty indicate teaching as their main activity (Provasnik & Planty, 2008). Moreover, faculty find the greatest satisfaction in their teaching (Cohen et al., 2014). With an average teaching load of five 3-hour courses per term (Townsend & Twombly, 2007), community college faculty have little to no time to engage in scholarly learning. For example, a five-five teaching load limits faculty from engaging in activities that may in fact help them discover and use more effective instructional approaches (Braxton, 2015). High teaching loads also preclude faculty from serving as faculty mentors for undergraduate research, which supports student learning and promotes student retention and student engagement (Cejda & Hensel, 2009; Kuh, 2008). Heavy teaching loads also stifle collaborations with both internal and external constituents.

Narrow Views of Scholarship

As discussed earlier, the role of research/scholarship at the community college has generated two perspectives: research is integral to good teaching, and research detracts from good teaching (Prager, 2003; Tinberg et al., 2007; Vaughan, 1988). Administrators and faculty alike share these views. While discussing the importance of the scholarship of teaching in the community college, Tinberg et al. (2007) stated:

> *While logic would suggest that teaching-centered institutions such as two-year colleges would welcome any national movement that paid serious attention to classroom instruction, the reality is otherwise. Where the fight at research-centered universities and colleges is to valorize teaching as a legitimate subject of scholarship and research, the struggle at two-year colleges is to convince faculty and administrators that intellectual inquiry and scholarly exchange are activities appropriate to the mission of the institutions. (para. 5)*

The central issue here is the definition and understanding of research/scholarship. Although Boyer (1990) proposed an expanded definition of research/scholarship, original research, or what he termed the "scholarship of discovery" (p. 17), continues to dominate the discourse. These narrow views promote a "hostility" (Palmer, 1992, p. 63) toward research/scholarship at the community college. This hostile or unreceptive attitude is grounded in ideas that scholarship pulls faculty away from their work with students (Palmer, 2015; Tinberg et al., 2007). However, as highlighted throughout this chapter, students are very much involved in the scholarly learning activities of faculty, even with limited resources and infrastructures. Further, although some faculty may not be interested in engaging in research/scholarship, others may hesitate to identify their efforts as such, either because they have adopted a narrow definition/view of research or because they fear how faculty colleagues and/or administrators will receive and reward their work, if at all (Braxton et al., 2015).

Limited Resources and Infrastructures

In addition to heavy teaching loads and narrow views of scholarship, community college faculty have limited access to resources and infrastructures that foster scholarly learning (Braxton et al., 2015; Terosky & Gonzales, 2016; Toth, 2014). For example, underresourced institutions such as community colleges have less funding to support faculty conference travel, which is one of several ways faculty can expand their disciplinary knowledge as well as contribute to the advancement of their disciplines. Faculty scholarly learning at community colleges is further challenged by inadequate facilities and equipment (Braxton et al., 2015; Cejda & Hensel, 2009; Martinez, 2014; Terosky & Gonzales, 2016). Perez's (2003) work on undergraduate research at community colleges highlighted how given the lack of "appropriate facilities" to conduct research, "initially [faculty] mentors borrowed equipment from senior colleges that was often out of date or redundant" (p. 75). Necessary equipment was later purchased through external funding from the National Science Foundation. Martinez's (2014) study discussed similar findings.

Opportunities for Faculty Scholarly Learning at Community Colleges

Faculty face multiple barriers in their pursuit of scholarly learning at community colleges; however, there are various opportunities or ways in which community colleges can support faculty scholarly learning. Recommended supports highlighted in the literature include (a) reducing teaching loads, (b) expanding views of scholarship, and (c) enhancing resources and infrastructures.

Reducing Teaching Loads

As established previously, a five-five teaching load is not conducive to faculty scholarly learning. To this point, faculty should have the opportunity to seek course releases. This recommendation is particularly important for community colleges moving toward offering baccalaureate degrees and *expecting* faculty to "present and publish" (McKinney & Morris, 2010, p. 204). Reduced teaching loads or opportunities to receive course buyout may also support faculty efforts to secure extramural funding, which may help provide additional opportunities for teaching release and/or summer salary and address the lack of institutional resources and infrastructures (Braxton et al., 2015; Hagedorn, 2015; Martinez, 2014; Morest, 2015; Perez, 2003). Reduced teaching loads evidently call for colleges to expand their views of scholarship.

Expanding View of Scholarship

To support faculty scholarly learning, community college leaders, faculty, and funders must adopt an expanded view of scholarship. Rather than continuing to view/define scholarship as original research, understandings must expand to include the scholarship of teaching, scholarship of integration, and scholarship of engagement (Boyer, 1990). In addition to expanding views of scholarship, both faculty and administrators must work to see the clear connection and importance of scholarship in fulfilling the community college mission (Palmer, 2015; Tinberg, et al., 2007). The divide in conceptions and understandings of scholarship serves to restrict rather than advance the community college mission. Although participation in the scholarship of teaching can improve student learning (Sperling, 2003), both the scholarship of engagement and scholarship of integration can enhance the community colleges' contributions by deliberately and intentionally addressing pressing local social issues. Relatedly, an expanded view of scholarship also calls for existing reward systems to be revisited. In order for community college faculty to engage in scholarly activities, they must be reassured that their work, outside of teaching, will be valued. This is especially true for tenure-line faculty. Throughout this process, of course, administrators and faculty must consider faculty contracts/collective bargaining agreements. As suggested by Hensel and Cejda (2015) regarding undergraduate research, "collective bargaining units also will need to review contracts to eliminate sections that preclude or make difficult engagement in student/faculty collaborative research" (para. 18). Resources and infrastructures are also necessary to encourage faculty to pursue scholarly learning.

Enhancing Resources and Infrastructures

Although acknowledging the existence of financial challenges faced by community colleges, scholars hold that these institutions must still work to allocate resources toward structures that support faculty scholarly learning (Braxton et al., 2015; Martinez, 2014; Terosky & Gonzales, 2016). Although Terosky and Gonzales (2016) noted that some participants were willing to bear conference costs, and Toth (2014) highlighted how community college faculty adopted innovative approaches, such as the delegate model, to participate in conferences and remain engaged with their disciplines, colleges have the responsibility to provide these resources. After all, as previously noted, faculty engagement in scholarly learning benefits faculty, students, and communities alike (Terosky & Gonzales, 2016). Presently, professional associations are striving to include and support community college faculty by offering financial support for faculty travel and participation. For example, in 2013 the Geological Society of America offered 45 stipends for community college faculty with at least half-time appointments to participate in short courses. Similarly, external funding sources are helping faculty obtain necessary equipment or establish adequate facilities to carry out their work (Perez, 2003); nonetheless, there needs to be an institutional commitment to supporting the scholarly learning of faculty.

Conclusions and Implications

The work presented in this chapter counters commonly held assumptions regarding community college faculty and how they spend their time. The work presented here helps the field move beyond the simple characterization of community college faculty as teachers. Without a doubt, teaching is their main responsibility. In fact, "teaching is the centerpiece of community college faculty identity" (Townsend & Twombly, 2007, p. 53). However, they also engage, albeit to differing degrees, in scholarly learning activities in each of the four domains outlined by Boyer (1990). Community college faculty are not only consumers, but also producers of knowledge (Braxton, 2015; Terosky & Gonzales, 2016). Still, faculty members face several barriers to scholarly learning. Reducing teaching loads, expanding views of scholarship, and enhancing resources and infrastructures are necessary actions to support the scholarly learning of faculty within the community college context. Certainly, we recognize that these recommendations cannot be accomplished overnight and are likely to meet some form of resistance.

Therefore, to begin, we call on community college leaders to welcome and engage in conversations related to faculty scholarly learning. Doing so would be the first step in developing a clear understanding of faculty scholarly learning—a widely misunderstood concept—across various stakeholders. These conversations would in turn help create an awareness of the forms of scholarly learning taking place on campus and how scholarly learning figures into realizing the college mission. By linking faculty scholarly learning to institutional mission, leaders can then consider how to manage scarce resources to support scholarly learning.

One approach to help facilitate these conversations and develop an action plan is evaluative thinking (ET). As defined by Buckley, Archibald, Hargraves, and Trochim (2015), "evaluative thinking is critical thinking applied in the context of evaluation, motivated by an attitude of inquisitiveness and a belief in the value of evidence, that involves identifying assumptions, posing thoughtful questions, pursuing deeper understanding through reflection and perspective taking, and information decisions in preparation for action" (p. 378).

Ultimately, the goal of ET would be to help foster a culture that supports and rewards various forms of scholarly learning. Of particular importance is that these conversations and considerations be made with both contingent and noncontingent faculty members in mind. In sum, although we encourage faculty to continue supporting each other's scholarly learning through informal spaces, we maintain that community college leaders have the responsibility to create formal spaces for faculty to pursue their passions and professional commitments, especially when we consider the potential contributions of faculty scholarly learning to positive undergraduate outcomes. The next and final chapter provides a synthesis of key findings on faculty scholarly learning across the four institution types featured in this monograph including recommendations for practice and future research.

A Call to Action: Advancing the Study of Faculty Scholarly Learning

IN THIS FINAL chapter, we provide a synthesis of key findings on faculty scholarly learning across the four institution types featured in this monograph. The goal of this monograph is to offer—and facilitate—a conversation that prioritizes and expands our understanding of faculty members' scholarly learning across all institution types, as well as pushes back on commonly accepted notions about scholarly learning and institution types. This monograph can foster deliberate and thoughtful connections between faculty scholarly learning and their work, in hopes of better supporting organizational outcomes, initiatives, faculty development, and mission-related priorities within the current (and future) contextual realities.

Synthesis of Key Findings and Implications

We return to the guiding research questions to frame the synthesis of key findings. The first question is—*What does scholarly learning, as conceptualized by Neumann (2009a), look like at different institution types?* As noted throughout the third through sixth chapters, there are limited studies centered on faculty scholarly learning. Further, the majority of the studies featured in this monograph did not employ scholarly learning as a lens to understanding faculty work. In general, scholarly learning, as a concept, is often misunderstood and understudied. Likely, this is because it is a sophisticated concept that many find challenging to clearly define, measure, and assess (Gappa et al., 2007; Neumann et al., 2006; Sullivan, 1995). Although scholars like Neumann (2005a, 2009a) and Terosky and Gonzales (2016) have advanced definitions and research on scholarly learning, the complexity of the concept, and the time needed to unbundle said complexity makes it a challenging area of study that requires long-term study, which is not always appreciated in today's society (Gonzales, 2016; Harvey, 2005). Moreover, during an era of declining public trust in higher education and the professoriate (Henderson, 2011; Hermanowicz, 2009; O'Meara, 2007, 2015) other research areas, for example, studies on the financial costs of colleges/universities, garner more attention than faculty members' scholarly learning.

This monograph counters the current narrative on where scholarly learning takes place, and the types of activities faculty members engage in at particular types of institutions through a comprehensive and integrative review of the extant literature from 2000 to present. The studies included in this monograph applied a broad spectrum of methodological approaches and were drawn from both higher education literature (Braxton et al., 2006; Park & Braxton, 2013; Terosky & Gonzales, 2016) and discipline-specific literature (Rowell, 2010; Toth, 2014; Vitullo & Spalter-Roth, 2013).

As underscored by the work highlighted in this monograph, how faculty members engage "with a subject that means a great deal to them or to which they have committed themselves deeply throughout their lives" (Neumann, 2009a, p. 2), is guided, though not wholly determined, by the institutional type in which they are situated. Indeed, scholarly learning takes place beyond major research universities. Further, scholarly learning occurs in different genres and for different aims (Boyer, 1990; Braxton, 2015; Terosky & Gonzales, 2016; Tinberg, 1997). Findings centered on research university faculty engagement in the scholarship of discovery were unsurprising; however, we also found significant evidence of scholarly learning within this particular domain at LACs, regional comprehensive universities, and community colleges (Braxton, 2015; Cejda & Hensel, 2009; Gonzales & Terosky, 2016; Martinez, 2014; Terosky & Gonzales, 2016). Scholars such as Terosky and Gonzales (2016) and Martinez (2012, 2014), for example, highlighted community college faculty collaborating with colleagues and students on traditional/basic research. Terosky and Gonzales (2016) also found that community college and broad access LAC faculty constructed knowledge through the scholarships of teaching and engagement. Similarly, Braxton's (2015) special issue on Community College Faculty Scholarship in *New Directions for Community Colleges* documented community college faculty immersion in all four of Boyer's (1990) domains.

Our analysis, which applied both Neumann's (2009a) conceptual framing of scholarly learning and Boyer's (1990) work on different types of scholarship, reinforced the need to further explore faculty scholarly learning across all institution types. Although we learned of various ways scholarly learning takes place at research universities, comprehensive universities, LACs, and community colleges, additional insights regarding scholarly learning activities and how and to what extent scholarly learning is considered when contemplating faculty work would be beneficial for stakeholders within and outside of the academy given its significance to the core mission of higher education, as well as faculty work, reward systems, and motivation (Campbell & O'Meara, 2014; Hermanowicz, 2011; Neumann, 2009b). In light of the importance of faculty scholarly learning, we encourage researchers to explicitly employ scholarly learning as a lens to study faculty work. As emphasized previously, the work of Teroksy and Gonzales (2016) is the only study in our analysis that explicitly applied scholarly learning as a lens.

Moreover, of the four types of scholarship, we found the least amount of evidence or work focused on the scholarship of integration. As such, we recommend a closer examination of what this form of scholarship looks like. Additionally, there is a need for research that further explores faculty and administrator perspectives regarding faculty scholarly learning and each of the types of scholarship across institution types, which ultimately influence decisions about faculty roles and rewards. Another area of research that has yet to be thoroughly explored is faculty scholarly learning in MSIs, specifically historically Black colleges and universities, Hispanic-serving institutions, tribal colleges and universities, and Asian American and Native American Pacific Islander-serving institutions. Although we attempted to discuss what faculty scholarly learning looks like within MSIs across each of the four institution types highlighted in this monograph, limited literature was available. Their origin, history, commitment to community, and diverse students provide

TABLE 5
Barriers to Faculty Scholarly Learning by Institution Type

Institutional Type	Barriers		
Research universities	Value vs. reward	Increased competition/demands for productivity	Academic capitalism
Comprehensive universities	Workload challenges	Mission confusion	Lack of resources
Liberal arts colleges	Inaccurate assumptions about academic work	Inadequate faculty development supports	Disconnection between expectations and reward/incentive structures
Community colleges	Heavy teaching loads	Narrow views of scholarship	Limited resources and infrastructures

distinct and valuable opportunities for faculty scholarly learning (Ambler & Crazy Bull, 1997; Gonzales, 2015; Sydnor et al., 2010). Furthermore, the percentages of faculty of color within MSIs surpass the exceptionally low national average (Gasman & Conrad, 2013), and as such, MSIs are spaces that may cultivate new ways of knowing, thinking, and doing (Gonzales, 2015; Quijada-Cerecer, Ek, Alanis, & Murakami-Ramalho, 2011). In addition to exploring how and to what extent MSIs support faculty scholarly learning, future work might include examining the degree to which MSIs support scholarship across Boyer's four domains. Given their distinct missions, is one form of scholarship more prevalent and/or valued than another? Further, how do these values differ across institution types and MSI designation, if at all? For example, whereas HBCUs were created to educate and serve African American students and communities, HSIs are designated as such based on a full-time equivalent undergraduate student enrollment that is at least 25% Latino/Hispanic.

Within each institutional type, there are several barriers and opportunities to faculty scholarly learning that emerged from the literature, which were featured in the third through sixth chapters and are summarized in Tables 5 and 6. For the purposes of the following discussion, we return to the second guiding question of the monograph—*What contexts and/or supports hinder or*

TABLE 6
Opportunities for Faculty Scholarly Learning by Institution Type

Institutional Type	Opportunities		
Research Universities	Faculty engagement in high-impact practices	Increase opportunities for internal/external stakeholder collaboration	Foster service to institution/community
Comprehensive Universities	Broadening views of scholarship	Develop an infrastructure of support	
Liberal Arts Colleges	Redefine faculty learning	Modernize faculty development supports	Align policy and practice
Community Colleges	Reduce teaching loads	Expand views of scholarship	Enhance resources and infrastructures

help faculty members' scholarly learning at different institution types?—as a means of highlighting the common barriers to faculty scholarly learning across institution types as a necessary step to advancing the field, both in terms of research and practice.

Barriers to Scholarly Learning Across All Institution Types: Implications for Research

Although it is clear that faculty are engaged in scholarly learning across the four institution types highlighted in this monograph, it is also apparent that they face various barriers while pursuing scholarly learning. The third, and final guiding question—*What challenges are noted in the extant literature on faculty work around further study of or better understanding of faculty members' scholarly learning across institution types?*—facilitated the identification of common barriers to scholarly learning, which include (a) narrow views of and academic work and scholarship, (b) contradictory and unclear faculty evaluation and reward systems, (c) limited organizational support and infrastructures, and (d) workload issues. Although each barrier is discussed separately in the following subsections, it is important to note that they are interconnected and contribute to or exacerbate each other.

Narrow Views of Academic Work and Scholarship

As previously noted, faculty across all four institution types are engaged to some degree in Boyer's four domains of scholarship. Nonetheless, myopic assumptions about where and on what faculty members spend their time persist. For example, given the teaching missions of both LACs and community colleges, internal and external stakeholders often confine the faculty role entirely to that of the teacher (Baker et al., in press; Townsend & Twombly, 2007). A rather significant assumption is that all faculty "do" is teach. As such then, their passions must also rest solely in teaching. Subsequently, faculty are viewed as disconnected and/or uninterested in learning beyond developing and improving pedagogical and curricular practices (Tinberg, 1997). These uncritically assimilated assumptions about faculty work are likely to stymie rather than stimulate and support scholarly learning by misinforming decisions surrounding necessary support and infrastructures, which are often inadequate and misaligned with organizational and faculty professional goals (Gardner, 2013; Gonzales, 2012). Moreover, despite Boyer's (1990) call to expand the definition of scholarship, as documented in the literature, it continues to be primarily defined and understood in terms of traditional/basic research. For example, overall, the role of research/scholarship at the community college has generated two perspectives: (a) research is integral to good teaching, and (b) research detracts from good teaching (Prager, 2003; Tinberg et al., 2007; Vaughan, 1988). Vaughan (1988), an early and vocal proponent of community college faculty scholarship, asserted, "outstanding teaching requires constant learning and intellectual renewal that cannot exist without these essential elements of scholarship" (p. 28). However, "at worst," others view scholarship as an "abrogation of the institution's student-focused values" (Palmer, 2015, p. 38). A discernible difference between these perspectives is the definition of research and scholarship employed. Whereas Vaughan employs a broad definition of scholarship, research/scholarship is usually thought of as original research or what Boyer (1990) termed the "scholarship of discovery" (p. 17). How faculty and administrators across all institution types define scholarship and what shapes their definition of scholarship is worthy of further examination.

Contradictory and Unclear Faculty Evaluation and Reward Systems

Although colleges and universities are increasingly encouraging and claiming to value various forms of faculty work and scholarship, the rewards do not align (Byrne, 2014; Fairweather, 2005; Gonzales & Rincones, 2012; Rhoten, 2010). The scholarship of discovery continues to be regarded as the most valuable form of scholarship (Braxton et al., 2006), whereas the scholarship of engagement (O'Meara, 2002), integration (Gonzales & Rincones, 2012), and teaching continue to face questions regarding rigor and measurement. In fact, as noted earlier, the scholarships of teaching and engagement are unlikely to count toward promotion and tenure at many institutions (Braxton et al., 2002; Huber & Hutchings, 2005; O'Meara, 2005b; O'Meara & Rice, 2005; Walker et al., 2008). As highlighted in the literature, faculty members are engaged in various forms of scholarship; however, how this work is evaluated continues to be unclear (Cruz et al., 2013; O'Meara, 2002).

Limited Organizational Support and Infrastructures

Similar to assumptions regarding faculty work, there are assumptions about the kinds of support and infrastructures certain types of institutions offer. For example, given the mission of LACs and community colleges, it is assumed that the scholarship of teaching is being entirely and successfully sustained and promoted (Peters et al., 2008; Townsend & Twombly, 2007). However, as discussed in the fifth chapter, few LACs actively engage in truly support-ing the scholarship of teaching (Peters et al., 2008). Moreover, in community colleges the success of existing efforts is limited given a lack of leadership and minimal faculty participation—particularly among those who have the most to gain from such professional development opportunities (Murray, 2000, 2002). Organizational support and infrastructures are necessary to stimulate and sustain faculty scholarly learning (Neumann, 2009b; Terosky & Gon-zales, 2016). Infrastructures include but are not limited to funding, physi-cal facilities, equipment, and specialized support staff. However, the lack of sufficient support and infrastructures to foster faculty work and scholarly learning has been widely documented, especially within striving contexts (Gardner, 2013; Gonzales, 2012; Martinez, 2014). Although faculty in striving colleges and universities face heightened expectations to produce research and publications (Henderson, 2007, 2011; O'Meara, 2007), the degree of available research-related resources does not match these demands (Doran, 2015; Gonzales, 2012).

As documented in the literature, unmet needs are especially common in low-resourced institutions such as community colleges and comprehensive universities. In addition to limited access to some of the tangible resources listed here, faculty may experience a deficiency in intangible resources/assets such as knowledge and support gained through faculty mentoring relationships. For instance, senior faculty may not have been required to engage in or produce high levels of scholarship for promotion and tenure purposes (Schuster & Finkelstein, 2006). Therefore, they may not have the capacity or desire to support the scholarly endeavors of junior faculty (Martinez, 2014; Palmer, 2015). To this point, it is vital to study faculty scholarly learning within striving contexts. Questions to consider in future studies include: How does institutional striving influence faculty scholarly learning? What do shifts in organizational missions mean for faculty scholarly learning?

Workload Issues

In relation to the challenges facing faculty members in the practice of scholarly learning, a number of macro-level issues shape faculty members' capacity to focus on their scholarly learning. For example, the public is increasingly demanding more accountability and efficiency from higher education, which often results in (a) reduced resources for faculty development and learning, and (b) increased calls for higher teaching loads, and rising demands that academics produce greater levels of publications and funding (Creamer, 1998; O'Meara, 2007; Gonzales, 2016). Gonzales (2016) points out that faculty members' work is "increasingly understood for its fiscal or cultural resource generation; and that evaluation of faculty work is contingent on their ability and willingness to self-survey or document" (para. 2) their work (see also Gonzales & Núñez, 2014). Similarly, decreasing governmental funding and the recession has resulted in reductions in tenure-track faculty lines and increases in contingent faculty, thereby heightening the workloads of those on the tenure track (Boyer et al., 2015; Ehrenberg & Zhang, 2005). As a result, Schuster and Finkelstein (2006) noted that faculty reported working 48.6 hours per week in 1998, which is an increase of 8.6 hours per week from 1984. In sum, because scholarly learning calls for time and focus, these macro-level influences of increased pressures to publish, diminishing funding for public institutions, and rising contingent hires disrupt and constrain the time and focus required for scholarly learning (Henderson, 2011; Hermanowicz, 2009; Neumann & Terosky, 2007; Neumann, 2009a; Terosky, Phifer, & Neumann, 2008).

Opportunities to Support Faculty Scholarly Learning Across All Institution Types: Implications for Research

Administrators and faculty colleagues alike are positioned to foster the enactment and advancement of scholarly learning. As noted by Neumann (2009a), "they may do that by leading in the creation of organizational settings that professors experience as encouraging of their scholarly learning—or at least, as not getting in its way" (p. 172). Several studies have recommended ways in which individual faculty members themselves and institutional leaders can support scholarly learning in the academic career. In Table 6 we note the opportunities for scholarly learning across institution types that emerged from the literature discussed in the third through sixth chapters.

Common opportunities for scholarly learning across institution types include (a) broadening or expanding views of scholarship, (b) revisiting workload and reward structures, and (c) improving organizational support and infrastructures. The recommendations we offer in this section are intended to lessen the barriers discussed in previous sections. Several of the barriers are interrelated; therefore, these recommendations should be considered collectively rather than severally. We discourage readers from considering these recommendations as standalone because such an approach presents an oversimplified response to supporting faculty scholarly learning.

Broadening or Expanding Views of Scholarship

As previously noted, despite Boyer's (1990) proposal for us to reconsider how we define scholarship more than 25 years ago, narrow views of what constitutes scholarship persist. Although all four domains of scholarship have attained some level of institutionalization (Braxton et al., 2002), the scholarship of discovery continues to be the most regarded form of scholarship (Boyer, 1990; Fairweather, 2005; Henderson, 2009). To date, it is valued and rewarded above any other form of scholarship, particularly at research universities, and increasingly among striving regional comprehensives.

Broadening views of scholarship, for one, would include openness to cross-disciplinarity, which "involves acts of boundary crossing—possibly boundary blurring—among people, thoughts, disciplinary, and other knowledge communities, departments and other organizational units, and other social groupings" (Neumann, 2009a, p. 195). As noted by Gonzales and Rincones (2012), several stakeholder groups have called on universities to approach education in more interdisciplinary ways (Albert 2002; Campbell, 2005; Hora, 2007). However, the academy continues to discourage this form of work in both real and perceived ways (Gonzales & Rincones, 2012; Rhoten, 2010). Rhoten (2010) provided a clear depiction of this scenario as follows:

> *We argue that despite "talking the talk" of cross-boundary collaboration, many universities are failing to "walk the walk". . . . many universities are simply adopting the interdisciplinary labels without adapting their disciplinary artifacts. The result has been problematic on two levels. Not only has the persistence of old structures created real or perceived disincentives to and penalties for pursuing interdisciplinary work. But, far more critically, the lack of systemic implementation taken in order to re-design and not just rename these structures. . . . has actually created initiatives that are inherently incapable of achieving the very goals they seek to accomplish. (p. 9)*

To this point, rather than causing faculty to work "overtime" (Gonzales & Rincones, 2012, p. 507) and view interdisciplinarity as a "risky route" (Byrne,

2014, n.p.), colleges and universities should intentionally seek to dismantle real and perceived barriers experienced by faculty in their pursuit of scholarly learning. Revisiting existing workloads and evaluation and reward structures and institutionalizing Boyer's perspective is one way to encourage and truly support scholarly learning.

Revisiting Workload and Reward Structures

Bearing the previous discussion in mind, it is clear that colleges and universities must revisit existing evaluation and reward structures, which are currently based on long-held values and a particular set of standards that privilege and legitimize certain kinds of knowledge and work over others (Delgado-Bernal & Villalpando, 2002; Gonzales & Terosky, 2016). As suggested by Gonzales and Terosky (2016), legitimacy is assigned to faculty whose professional identity and work revolves around traditional research and publication (Gonzales, 2012, 2015).

Although Boyer's *Scholarship Reconsidered* has been widely cited (Braxton et al., 2002) and both faculty and administrators report relying on it to inform discussions centered on faculty roles and rewards (Glassick et al., 1997; O'Meara, 2005b), the findings presented in this monograph underscore the need for colleges and universities to revisit *Scholarship Reconsidered* and reassess current definitions of scholarship. This recommendation proves beneficial for all institutions given the numerous benefits associated with encouraging multiple forms of scholarship, such as greater faculty satisfaction, better retention, improved reward systems, and enhanced institutional effectiveness (O'Meara, 2005b). Faculty should have the opportunity to pursue their passion and commitment to a subject matter in multiple ways without concern for whether or not it "will count" toward tenure.

Improving Resources and Infrastructure

The availability of resources and infrastructures to support both organizational and faculty professional goals is fundamental. Although financial constraints might limit resources and infrastructures, collaborations with internal and external stakeholders may help address these scarcities (Hagedorn, 2015; Morest, 2015). Extramural funding may support and provide a space for scholarly learning by providing opportunities for release time (Morest, 2015). At the same time, organizational infrastructures to help faculty secure these external sources of funding to carry out various forms of scholarship are needed.

Neumann (2009a rightly noted that "to understand how universities—and the leaders—can support professors' scholarly learning requires knowing which university structures, processes, and cultures engender professors' scholarly learning" (p. 172). In agreement with Neumann (2009a), we recommend that colleges and universities engage in self-study. Organizational self-study is encouraged to help colleges and universities assess which of their individual structures, processes, and cultural elements stimulate scholarly learning. Self-studies may be conducted at the organizational, college, and department levels. Findings might help inform future investment or divestment in existing structures or lead to the creation of new structures. Decisions should be driven by both quantitative and qualitative data and not based on some of the prevailing unexamined assumptions discussed earlier.

Future Directions for Research and Scholarship

In addition to the implications and recommendations for research and practice embedded in the discussion, this work has illuminated additional areas for future research. Although this monograph focused on institutional type as an organizational focus, appointment type and disciplinary/departmental context also influence faculty scholarly learning (Bloomgarden & O'Meara, 2007; Clark, 1987a, 1987b; O'Meara, 2005a; Tierney & Bensimon, 1996). To this point, future studies should consider what faculty scholarly learning looks like in distinctive disciplinary/departmental contexts as well as by appointment type (e.g., tenure track vs. nontenure track). This is particularly relevant given the new faculty majority across colleges and universities (Kezar, 2012; Kezar & Sam, 2010). Relatedly, we recommend large-scale nationwide surveys that derive key factors about faculty, faculty work, faculty matters, and the academic workplace. To help us provide an overview of faculty work-time allocation, we relied on 2016 FSSE data. FSSE is one of a few large-scale nationwide surveys that derives some of the key factors listed here.

Similar instruments include the HERI Faculty Survey administered by the Cooperative Institutional Research Program at the Higher Education Research Institute (https://heri.ucla.edu) and the National Study of Postsecondary Faculty (NSOPF) administered by the National Center for Education Statistics (https://nces.ed.gov/surveys/nsopf/). NSOPF is the most comprehensive study of faculty in higher education but has not been administered since the 2003–2004 cycle (https://nces.ed.gov/surveys/nsopf/). The FSSE and HERI are administered on an annual and triennial basis, respectively, but are available exclusively on a proprietary basis, making it challenging for the institution types we know less about to participate.

Finally, future research should also consider how scholarly learning is influenced in graduate school. Exploring the extent to which aspiring faculty are encouraged to pursue their passion and commitment to a particular subject matter is an important inquiry. Socialization to the academic profession occurs in graduate school (Austin, 2002; Gardner, 2010). Within this space, aspiring faculty learn the expectations as well as the implicit and explicit cultural rules of the academic profession. Once faculty achieve their professional aspirations, they will actively engage in shaping and transforming existing reward systems that advance faculty. To this point, future research should consider the role graduate programs play in reproducing narrow definitions of scholarship. Another area of exploration is how and to what extent graduate programs promote Boyer's four domains, if at all.

Concluding Thoughts

The purpose of this monograph was to understand the scholarly learning of faculty members across the full range of institution types in U.S. higher education better. We emphasized two areas of study in academic careers: scholarly learning and institutional type. Our emphasis on institution types was based on the lack of knowledge about the scholarly learning of faculty members employed at institutions that are not characterized as major research universities or well-resourced institutions (Dougherty, 2011; Schuster & Finkelstein, 2006). The work discussed in this monograph countered some of the commonly held assumptions regarding the forms scholarly learning that occur across institution types. Based on these works we identified challenges and opportunities for scholarly learning, as well as highlighted implications for research and practice. It is our hope that this monograph will help set a practice and research agenda centered on faculty scholarly learning, which is central to the core mission of higher education.

References

Abbott, A. (2001). *The chaos of disciplines*. Chicago, IL: University of Chicago.

Acevedo-Gil, N., Santos, R., & Solorzano, D. (2014). Examining a rupture in the Latina/o college pipeline: Developmental education in California community colleges. *Perspectivas: Issues in Higher Education Policy and Practice, 3*(3).

Åkerlind, G. S. (2005). Academic growth and development-How do university academics experience it? *Higher Education, 50*(1), 1–32.

Albert, M. (2002, Sept./Oct.). The relevance of Pierre Bourdieu's social theory for the study of scientific knowledge production. *Canadian Journal of Sociology Online*. Retrieved from http://citeseerx.ist.psu.edu/viewdoc/summary?doi=10.1.1.453.6122.

Altbach, P. G., & Salmi, J. (Eds.). (2011). *The road to academic excellence: The making of world-class research universities*. Washington, DC: World Bank Publications.

Altbach, P. G., Gumport, P. J., & Johnstone, D. B. (2001), *In defense of American higher education*. Baltimore: Johns Hopkins University Press.

Ambler, M. (1999). Diné College students research diabetes for their people. *Tribal College, 11*(1), 18.

Ambler, M., & Crazy Bull, C. (1997). Survey: Tribal colleges deeply involved in research. *Tribal College Journal of American Indian Higher Education, 9*(1), 13–15.

American Association of Community Colleges. (n.d.). Mission. Retrieved from http://www.aacc.nche.edu/AboutCC/history/Pages/mission.aspx

Arreola, R. A. (2000). *Developing a comprehensive faculty evaluation system: A handbook for college faculty and administrators on designing and operating a comprehensive faculty evaluation system*. Boston, MA: Anker Publishing Company.

Austin, A. E. (2002). Preparing the next generation of faculty: Graduate school as socialization to the academic career. *Journal of Higher Education, 73*(1), 94–122.

Austin, A. E., & McDaniels, M. (2006). Using doctoral education to prepare faculty to work within Boyer's four domains of scholarship. In J. M. Braxton (Ed.), *New Directions for*

Institutional Research: No. 129. Analyzing faculty work and rewards: Using Boyer's four do-mains of scholarship (pp. 51–65). San Francisco, CA: Jossey-Bass.

Ayers, D. F. (2005). Neoliberal ideology in community college mission statements: A critical discourse analysis. *Review of Higher Education, 28*(4), 527–549.

Bailey, T. (2009). Challenge and opportunity: Rethinking the role and function of develop-mental education in community college. In A. C. Bueschel & A. Venezia, *New Directions for Community Colleges: No. 145. Policies and practices to improve student preparation and success* (pp. 11–30). San Francisco, CA: Jossey-Bass.

Bailey, T. R., Jaggars, S. S., & Jenkins, D. (2015). *Redesigning America's community colleges.* Cambridge, MA: Harvard University Press.

Baker, V. L., & Baldwin, R. G. (2015). Liberal arts colleges in the 21st century: An integra-tive approach to understanding organizational change and evolution in higher education. *Innovative Higher Education, 40*(3), 247–261.

Baker, V. L., Baldwin, R. G., & Makker, S. (2012). Where are they now? Revisiting Breneman's study of liberal arts colleges. *Liberal Education, 98*(3), 48–53.

Baker, V. L., Greer, J., Lunsford, L. G., Pifer, M. J., & Ihas, D. (2016). Documenting the aspi-ration gap in institutional language about undergraduate research, scholarship, and creative work. *Innovative Higher Education*, 1–17. https://doi.org/10.1007/s10755-016-9372-9

Baker, V. L., Lunsford, L. G., & Pifer, M. J. (in press). *Developing faculty in liberal arts colleges: Aligning individual needs and organizational goals.* New Brunswick, NJ: Rutgers University Press

Baker, V. L., Pifer, M. J., & Lunsford, L. G. (2016, November). *Transforming faculty devel-opment in the 21st century liberal arts college.* Paper presented at the annual meeting of the Professional and Organizational Development Network in Higher Education, Louisville, KY.

Baldwin, R. G., & Baker, V. L. (2009, July 9). The case of the disappearing liberal arts college. *Inside Higher Ed.* Retrieved from https://www.insidehighered.com/views/2009/07/09/baldwin

Bardo, J. W. (Ed.). (1990). *Defining the missions of AASCU institutions.* Washington, DC: American Association of State Colleges and Universities.

Beach, A. L., Sorcinelli, M. D., Austin, A. E., & Rivard, J. K. (2016). *Faculty development in the age of evidence: Current practices, future imperatives.* Sterling, VA: Stylus Publishing.

Becker, W. E., & Andrews, M. L. (2010). *The scholarship of teaching and learning in higher education: Contributions of research universities.* Bloomington, IN: Indiana University Press.

Bemmel, E. P., Floyd, D. L., & Bryan, V. C. (2008). Perceptions and reflections of admin-istrators: Community colleges transitioning to baccalaureate colleges. *Community College Journal of Research and Practice, 33*, 151–176.

Bentley, P. J., & Kyvik, S. (2013). Individual differences in faculty research time allocations across 13 countries. *Research in Higher Education, 54*(3), 329–348.

Blackburn, R. T., & Lawrence, J. H. (1995). *Faculty at work: Motivation, expectation, satisfac-tion.* Baltimore, MD: Johns Hopkins University Press.

Bloomgarden, A. H., & O'Meara, K. A. (2007). Faculty role integration and community en-gagement. *Michigan Journal of Community Service Learning, 13*(2), 5–18.

Bogue, E. G., & Aper, J. (2000). *Exploring the heritage of American higher education: The evo-lution of philosophy and policy.* Phoenix, AZ: Oryx.

Bowen, W. (2016). *Issues facing major research universities at a time of stress AND opportunity*. Keynote address for 250th Anniversary Presidential Symposium: The Future of the Research University, Rutgers University. Retrieved from http://www.sr.ithaka.org/publications/issues-facing-major-research-universities-at-a-time-of-stress-and-opportunity/

Boyer, E. L. (1990). *Scholarship reconsidered: Priorities of the professoriate*. New York, NY: Carnegie Foundation for the Advancement of Teaching.

Boyer, E. L., Moser, D., Ream, T. C., & Braxton, J. M. (2015). *Scholarship reconsidered: Priorities of the professoriate*. Hoboken, NJ: John Wiley & Sons.

Bozeman, B., & Gaughan, M. (2011). Job satisfaction among university faculty: Individual, work, and institutional determinants. *Journal of Higher Education, 82*(2), 154–186.

Braxton, J. M., Luckey, W., & Helland, P. (2002). *Institutionalizing a broader view of scholarship through Boyer's four domains*. Hoboken, NJ: Jossey-Bass.

Braxton, J. M., Luckey, W. T., & Helland, P. A. (2006). Ideal and actual value patterns toward domains of scholarship in three types of colleges and universities. In J. M. Braxton (Ed.), *New Directions for Institutional Research: No. 129. Analyzing faculty work and rewards: Using Boyer's four domains of scholarship* (pp. 67–76). San Francisco, CA: Jossey-Bass.

Braxton, J. M. (Ed.). (2015). *New Directions for Community Colleges: No. 171. Community college faculty scholarship*. San Francisco, CA: Jossey-Bass.

Braxton, J. M., & Lyken-Segosebe, D. (2015). Community college faculty engagement in Boyer's domains of scholarship. In J. M. Braxton (Ed.), *New Directions for Community Colleges: No. 171. Community college faculty scholarship* (pp. 7–14). San Francisco, CA: Jossey-Bass.

Breneman, D.W. (1990). Are we losing our liberal arts colleges?" *AAHE Bulletin, 4*(2), 3–6.

Brint, S. (2005). Creating the future: "New directions" in American research universities. *Minerva, 43*(1), 23–50.

Brint, S. (2011). Focus on the classroom: Movements to reform college teaching and learning, 1980–2008. In J. Hermanowicz (Ed.), *The American academic profession: Transformation in contemporary higher education* (pp. 44–91). Baltimore, MD: John Hopkins University Press.

Brown, G. A., Bull, J., & Pendlebury, M. (2013). *Assessing student learning in higher education*. New York, NY: Routledge.

Buckley, J., Archibald, T., Hargraves, M., & Trochim, W. M. (2015). Defining and teaching evaluative thinking: Insights from research on critical thinking. *American Journal of Evaluation, 36*(3), 375–388.

Buller, J. (2009). *The essential college professor: A practical guide to an academic career*. San Francisco, CA: Jossey-Bass.

Byrne, S. (2014, February 19). Interdisciplinary research: Why it's seen as a risky route. *The Guardian*. Retrieved from https://www.theguardian.com/higher-education-network/blog/2014/feb/19/interdisciplinary-research-universities-academic-careers

Campbell, L. M. (2005). Overcoming obstacles to interdisciplinary research. *Conservation Biology, 19*(2), 574–577.

Campbell, C. M., & O'Meara, K. (2014). Faculty agency: Departmental contexts that matter in faculty careers. *Research in Higher Education, 55*(1), 49–74.

Cantwell, B., Kauppinen, I., & Slaughter, S. (2014). *Academic capitalism in the age of globalization*. Baltimore, MD: Johns Hopkins University Press.

Cariaga-Lo, L., Dawkins, P. W., Enger, R., Schotter, A., & Spence, C. (2010). Supporting the development of the professoriate. *Peer Review, 12*(3), 19.

Carnegie Classification of Institutions of Higher Education. (2015). *Distribution of institutions and enrollments by classification category* [Data file]. Retrieved from http://carnegieclassifications.iu.edu/2010/summary/basic.php

Carnegie Classification of Institutions of Higher Education. (2016). About the Carnegie Classification™. Retrieved from http://carnegieclassifications.iu.edu/

Cataldi, E. F., Fahimi, M., Bradburn, E. M., & Zimbler, L. (2005). 2004 National Study of Postsecondary Faculty (NSOPF: 04) Report on Faculty and Instructional Staff in Fall 2003. ED TAB. NCES 2005–172. *US Department of Education.*

Cejda, B. D., & Hensel, N. (2009). An overview of undergraduate research in community colleges. *Undergraduate research at community colleges.* Washington, DC: Council on Undergraduate Research. Retrieved from http://www.cur.org/urcc/

Chism, N. V., Lees, N. D., & Evenbeck, S. (2002). Faculty development for teaching innovation. *Liberal Education, 88*(3), 34–41.

Chopp, R., Frost, S., & Weiss, D. H. (Eds.). (2013). *Remaking college: Innovation and the liberal arts.* Baltimore, MD: Johns Hopkins University Press.

Clark, B. R. (1987a). *The academic life: Small worlds, different worlds.* Princeton, NJ: Carnegie Foundation for the Advancement of Teaching.

Clark, B. R. (Ed.). (1987b). *The academic profession: National, disciplinary, and institutional settings.* Berkeley, CA: University of California Press.

Clark, B. R. (1997). Small worlds, different worlds: The uniquenesses and troubles of American academic professions. *Daedalus, 126*(4), 21–42.

Clark, B. R. (1989). The academic life small worlds, different worlds. *Educational Researcher, 18*(5), 4–8.

Cohen, A. M., & Brawer, F. B. (1977). *The two-year college instructor today.* New York, NY: Praeger Special Studies.

Cohen, A. M., Brawer, F. B., & Kisker, C. B. (2014). *The American community college* (6th ed.). San Francisco, CA: Jossey-Bass.

Colbeck, C. L., & Wharton-Michael, P. (2006). Individual and organizational influences on faculty members' engagement in public scholarship. In R. A. Eberly & J. Cohen (Eds.), *New Directions for Teaching and Learning: No. 105. A laboratory for public scholarship and democracy* (pp. 17–26). San Francisco, CA: Jossey-Bass.

Cole, J. R. (2016, September 20). The triumph of America's research university. *The Atlantic.* Retrieved from http://www.theatlantic.com/education/archive/2016/09/the-triumph-of-americas-research-university/500798/

Conrad, C., & Gasman, M. (2015). *Educating a diverse nation.* Boston, MA: Harvard University Press.

Cooke, N. J., Gorman, J. C., Duran, J. L., & Taylor, A. R. (2007). Team cognition in experienced command-and-control teams. [*Journal of Experimental Psychology: Applied, 13,* 146–157.

Coser, L. A. (1974). *Greedy institutions: Patterns of undivided commitment.* New York, NY: Free Press.

Creamer, E. G. (1998). Assessing faculty publication productivity: Issues of equity. [*ASHE-ERIC Higher Education Report, 26*(2)]. Washington, DC: George Washington University Graduate School of Education and Human Development.

Creamer, E. G. (2005). Promoting the effective evaluation of collaboratively produced scholarship: A call to action. In E. G. Creamer & L. R. Lattuca (Eds.), *New Directions for Teach-*

ing and Learning: No. 102. Advancing faculty learning through interdisciplinary collaboration (pp. 85–98). San Francisco, CA: Jossey-Bass.

Creamer, E. G., & Lattuca, L. R. (Eds.). (2005). *New Directions for Teaching and Learning: No. 102. Advancing faculty learning through interdisciplinary collaboration*. San Francisco, CA: Jossey-Bass.

Cruz, L., Ellern, G. D., Ford, G., Moss, H., & White, B. (2013). Navigating the boundaries of the scholarship of engagement at a regional comprehensive university. *Journal of Higher Education Outreach and Engagement, 17*(1), 3–26.

D'Avanzo, C. (2009, Spring). Supporting faculty through a new teaching and learning center. *Peer Review, 11*(2), 22–25.

Delgado-Bernal, D., & Villalpando, O. (2002). An apartheid of knowledge in academia: The struggle over the "legitimate" knowledge of faculty of color. *Equity & Excellence in Education, 35*(2), 169–180.

Dewey, J. (1902). The child and the curriculum. In R. D. Archambault (Ed.), *John Dewey on education: Selected writings* (pp. 339–358). Chicago, IL: University of Chicago Press.

Dey, E. L., Milem, J. F., & Berger, J. B. (1997). Changing patterns of publication productivity: Accumulative advantage or institutional isomorphism? *Sociology of Education, 70*(4), 308–323.

Diamond, R. M. (1999). *Aligning faculty rewards with institutional mission: Statements, policies, and guidelines*. Bolton, MA: Anker.

Diné College hosts diabetes research students. (2001, November 15). Tribal College: Journal of American Indian Higher Education, *13*(3). Retrieved from http://tribalcollegejournal.org/dine-college-hosts-diabetes-research-students/

Disappointing progress in enrollments of low-income students at America's most selective colleges and universities. (2009). Journal of Blacks in Higher Education. Retrieved from http://www.jbhe.com/features/61_lowincome.html.

Doran, E. (2015). Negotiating access and tier one aspirations: The historical evolution of a striving Hispanic-serving institution. *Journal of Hispanic Higher Education, 14*(4), 1–12.

Dougherty, K. J. (2011). The community college: The origins, impacts, and futures of a contradictory institution. In J. Ballantine & J. Spade (Eds.), *Sociology of education* (4th ed.). Upper Saddle River, NJ: Prentice-Hall.

Dougherty, K. J., & Townsend, B. K. (2006). Community college missions: A theoretical and historical perspective. In B. K. Townsend & K. J. Dougherty (Eds.), *New Directions for Community Colleges: No. 136. Community college missions in the 21st century* (pp. 5–13). San Francisco, CA: Jossey-Bass.

Duffy, D. K. (2006). Communities of practice: Pooling educational resources to foster the scholarship of teaching and learning. *Community College Journal of Research and Practice, 30*, 151–152.

Eagan, K. (2007). A national picture of part-time community college faculty: Changing trends in demographics and employment characteristics. In R. L. Wagoner (Ed.), *New Directions for Community Colleges: No. 140. The current landscape and changing perspectives of part-time faculty* (pp. 5–14). San Francisco, CA: Jossey-Bass.

Eagan, M. K., Jr., Sharkness, J., Hurtado, S., Mosqueda, C. M., & Chang, M. J. (2011). Engaging undergraduates in science research: Not just about faculty willingness. *Research in Higher Education, 52*(2), 151–177.

Eddy, P. L. (2010). *Community college leadership: A multidimensional model for leading change.* Sterling, VA: Stylus Publishing.

Eddy, P. L. (2012). (Ed.). *New Directions for Community Colleges: No. 159. Leading for the future: Alignment of AACC competencies with practice.* San Francisco, CA: Jossey-Bass.

Ehrenberg, R. G., & Zhang, L. (2005). The changing nature of faculty employment. In R. Clark & J. Ma (Eds.), *Recruitment, retention, and retirement in higher education: Building and managing the faculty of the future* (pp. 32–52). Northhampton, MA: Edward Elgar.

Entwistle, N., & Ramsden, P. (2015). *Understanding student learning.* New York, NY: Routledge.

Etzkowitz, H. (2003). Research groups as "quasi-firms": The invention of the entrepreneurial university. *Research Policy, 32*(1), 109–121.

Fain, P. (2013, September 27). California's evolving master plan. *Inside Higher Ed.* Retrieved from http://www.insidehighered.com/news/2013/09/27/two-year-colleges-california-mull-bachelors-degrees

Fairweather, J. S. (2005). Beyond the rhetoric: Trends in the relative value of teaching and research in faculty salaries. *Journal of Higher Education, 76*(4), 401–422.

Fayne, H. R., & Ortquist-Ahrens, L. (2006). Entry-year teachers inside and outside of the academy. *College Teaching, 54*(4), 320–323.

Ferrall, V. E., Jr. (2011). *Liberal arts at the brink.* Cambridge, MA: Harvard University Press.

Floyd, D. L. (2005). The community college baccalaureate in the U.S.: Models, programs, and issues. In D. L. Floyd, M. L. Skolnik, & K. P. Walker (Eds.), *The community college baccalaureate: Emerging trends & policy issues* (pp. 25–47). Sterling, VA: Stylus.

Formicola, A. (2007). Institutional challenges of interdisciplinary research centers. *Journal of Research Administration, 38*(2), 28.

Freire P. (1970). *Pedagogy of the oppressed.* New York, NY: Continuum Publishing.

Frost, S. H., & Teodorescu, D. (2001). Teaching excellence: How faculty guided change at a research university. *Review of Higher Education, 24*(4), 397–415.

Fugate, A. L., & Amey, M. J. (2000). Career stages of community college faculty: A qualitative analysis of their career paths, roles, and development. *Community College Review, 28*(1), 1–22.

Gandara, P., & Cuellar, M. (2016, July 11). *The baccalaureate in the California community college: Current challenges and future prospects.* Los Angeles, CA: The Civil Rights Project. Retrieved from https://www.civilrightsproject.ucla.edu/research/college-access/underrepresented-students/the-baccalaureate-in-the-california-community-college-current-challenges-future-prospects/CA-CC-BA-report-070616.pdf

Gappa, J. M., Austin, A. E., & Trice, A. G. (2007). *Rethinking faculty work: Higher education's strategic imperative.* San Francisco, CA: Jossey-Bass.

Gardner, S. K. (2010). Keeping up with the Joneses: Socialization and culture in doctoral education at one striving institution. *Journal of Higher Education, 81*, 658–679.

Gardner, S. K. (2013). Women faculty departures from a striving institution: Between a rock and a hard place. *Review of Higher Education, 36*(3), 349–370.

Gasman, M., Baez, B., & Turner, C. S. V. (Eds.). (2008). *Understanding minority-serving institutions.* Albany, NY: State University of New York Press.

Gasman, M., & Conrad, C. F. (2013). *Minority serving institutions: Educating all students.* Philadelphia, PA: Penn Center for Minority Serving Institutions, Graduate School of Education, University of Pennsylvania. Retrieved from http://www.gse.upenn.edu/pdf/cmsi/msis_educating_all_students.pdf

Geiger, R. L. (2005). The ten generations of American higher education. In P. G. Altbach, R. O. Berdahl, & P. J. Gumport (Eds.), *American higher education in the twenty-first century: Social, political, and economic challenges* (2nd ed., pp. 38–70). Baltimore, MD: Johns Hopkins University Press.

Gillespie, K., & Robertson, D. L. (2010). *A guide to faculty development.* Hoboken, NJ: John Wiley & Sons.

Givens, T. E. (2011, June 29). The professor as entrepreneur. *Inside Higher Ed.* Retrieved from https://www.insidehighered.com/advice/running/essay_on_impact_of_texas_higher_ed_debates_on_faculty

Glassick, C. E., Huber, M. T., & Maeroff, G. I. (1997). *Scholarship assessed: Evaluation of the professoriate.* San Francisco, CA: Jossey-Bass.

Goldrick-Rab, S. (2010). Challenges and opportunities for improving community college student success. *Review of Educational Research, 80*(3), 437–469.

Gonzales, L. D. (2012). Responding to mission creep: Faculty members as cosmopolitan agents. *Higher Education, 64*(3), 337–353.

Gonzales, L. D. (2013). Faculty sensemaking and mission creep: Interrogating institutionalized ways of knowing and doing legitimacy. *Review of Higher Education, 36*(2), 179–209.

Gonzales, L. D. (2015). A horizon of possibilities for Hispanic Serving Institutions: Using funds of knowledge scholarship to reshape the production and legitimization of knowledge within academia. In S. Hurtado, A. M. Núñez, & E. Calderon-Galdeano (Eds.), *Hispanic-serving institutions: Advancing research and transformative practice* (pp. 121–235). New York, NY: Routledge.

Gonzales, L. D. (2016, February 23). Transcending macro to micro: Lines of research that can assist in understanding the manifestation of neoliberalism in the lives of faculty [Blog post]. Retrieved from http://aeradivisionj.blogspot.com/2016/02/transcending-macro-to-micro-lines-of.html

Gonzales, L. D., & Ayers, D. F. (in press). The convergence of institutional logics and the normalization of emotional labor: A new theoretical approach for considering the expectations and experiences of community college faculty. *Review of Higher Education.*

Gonzales, L. D., & Núñez, A. M. (2014). Ranking regimes and the production of knowledge in academia: (Re)shaping faculty work. *Education Policy Analysis Archives, 22*, 1–23.

Gonzales, L. D., & Rincones, R. (2012). Interdisciplinary scholars: Negotiating legitimacy at the core and from the margins. *Journal of Further and Higher Education, 36*(4), 495–518.

Gonzales, L. D., & Terosky, A. L. (2016, May). From the faculty perspective: Defining, earning, and maintaining legitimacy across academia. *Teachers College Record, 18*(6). Retrieved from http://www.tcrecord.org/library/Abstract.asp?ContentId=20805

Gornall, L., & Salisbury, J. (2012). Compulsive working, "hyperprofessionality" and the unseen pleasures of academic work. *Higher Education Quarterly, 66*(2), 135–154.

Graham, H. D., & Diamond, N. (1997). *The rise of American research universities: Elites and challengers in the postwar era.* Baltimore, MD: Johns Hopkins University Press.

Grubb, W. N., & Lazerson, M. (2005). Vocationalism in higher education: The triumph of the education gospel. *Journal of Higher Education, 76*(1), 1–25.

Gulbrandsen, M., & Smeby, J. C. (2005). Industry funding and university professors' research performance. *Research Policy, 34*(6), 932–950.

Hagedorn, L. S. (2015). A national initiative of teaching, researching, and dreaming: Community college faculty research in "Achieving the Dream" colleges. In J. M. Braxton (Ed.), *New Directions for Community Colleges: No. 171. Community college faculty scholarship* (pp. 49–62). San Francisco, CA: Jossey-Bass.

Hansen, D. T. (1994). Teaching and the sense of vocation. *Educational Theory, 44*(3), 259–275.

Hansen, D. T. (1995). *The call to teach.* New York, NY: Teachers College Press.

Harvey, D. (2005). *A brief history of neoliberalism.* New York, NY: Oxford University Press.

Heffner, G. G., Curry, J. M., & Beversluis, C. D. (2006). Transforming liberal arts education through engaged scholarship. *Journal of Higher Education Outreach and Engagement, 11*(1), 119–132.

Henderson, B. B. (2007). *Teaching at the people's university: An introduction to the state comprehensive university.* San Francisco, CA: Jossey Bass/Anker Series.

Henderson, B. B. (2009). The work of the people's university. *Teacher Scholar: The Journal of the State Comprehensive University, 1*(1), 5–29.

Henderson, B. B. (2011). Publishing patterns at state comprehensive universities: The changing nature of faculty work and the quest for status. *Journal of the Professoriate, 5*(2), 35–66.

Henderson, B. B., & Buchanan, H. E. (2007). The scholarship of teaching and learning: A special niche for faculty at comprehensive universities? *Research in Higher Education, 48*, 523–543.

Henderson, B. B., & Kane, W. D. (1991). Caught in the middle: Faculty and institutional status and quality in state comprehensive universities. *Higher Education, 22*, 339–350.

Hensel, N. H., & Cejda, B. D. (2015). Embedding undergraduate research in the community college curriculum. *Peer Review, 17*(4), 27.

Hermanowicz, J. C. (1998). *The stars are not enough: Scientists—their passions and professions.* Chicago, IL: University of Chicago Press.

Hermanowicz, J. C. (2009). *Lives in science: How institutions affect academic careers.* Chicago, IL: University of Chicago Press.

Hermanowicz, J. C. (Ed.). (2011). *The American academic profession: Transformation in contemporary higher education.* Baltimore, MD: Johns Hopkins University Press.

Holley, K. A. (2015). Doctoral education and the development of an interdisciplinary identity. *Innovations in Education and Teaching International, 52*(6), 642–652.

Holley, K. (2009). The challenge of an interdisciplinary curriculum: A cultural analysis of a doctoral-degree program in neuroscience. *Higher Education, 58*(2), 241–255.

Holmgren, R. A. (2005). Teaching partners: Improving teaching and learning by cultivating a community of practice. In S. Chadwick-Blossey & D. R. Robertson (Eds.), *To improve the academy: Vol. 23. Resources for faculty, instructional, and organizational development* (pp. 211–219). Bolton, MA: Anker.

Hora, M. T. (2007). *Analyzing cultural processes in higher education: STEM and education faculty collaboration in teacher education.* Paper presented at the annual meeting of the American Educational Research Association, Chicago, Illinois. Retrieved from http://hub.mspnet.org/media/data/Hora_AERA_2007_Paper.pdf?media_000000006161.pdf

Huber, M. (2002). Faculty evaluation and the development of academic careers. In C. Colbeck (Ed.), *Evaluating faculty performance.* San Francisco, CA: Jossey-Bass.

Huber, M. T., & Hutchings, P. (2005). *The advancement of learning: Building the teaching commons*. San Francisco, CA: Jossey-Bass.

Hughes, A. (2014, August 11). Earning tenure at small colleges. *Inside Higher Ed*. Retrieved from https://www.insidehighered.com/advice/2014/08/11/essay-earning-tenure-small-liberal-arts-colleges

Indiana University Center for Postsecondary Research. (2015). *The Carnegie Classification of Institutions of Higher Education, 2015 edition*. Bloomington, IN: Author.

Indiana University. (2016). Faculty Survey of Student Engagement. Retrieved from http://fsse.indiana.edu/

Inside Higher Ed. (2015). *A guide for applying to jobs at selective liberal arts colleges*. Retrieved from https://www.insidehighered.com/advice/2015/10/23/advice-getting-job-selective-liberal-arts-college-essay

Jacobs, J. A. (2014). *In defense of disciplines: Interdisciplinarity and specialization in the research university*. Chicago, IL: University of Chicago Press.

Jaeger, A. J. (2008). Contingent faculty and student outcomes. *Academe, 94*(6), 42.

Jenkins, R. (2012). What graduate students want to know about community college, part I. *Chronicle of Higher Education*. Retrieved from http://www.chronicle.com/article/What-Graduate-Students-Want-to/131600/

Jenkins, D., & Fink, J. (2016). *Tracking transfer: New measures of institutional and state effectiveness in helping community college students attain bachelor's degrees*. New York: Community College Research Center, Teachers College, Columbia University. Retrieved from http://ccrc.tc.columbia.edu/media/k2/attachments/tracking-transfer-institutional-state-effectiveness.pdf

Johnson, D. R. (2012). Technological change and professional control in the professoriate. *Science, Technology & Human Values, 38*(1), 126–149. https://doi.org/0162243911430236

Johnson, W. B. (2007). *On being a mentor: A guide for higher education faculty*. Mahwah, NJ: Erlbaum.

Kane, R., Sandretto, S., & Heath, C. (2002). Telling half the story: A critical review of research on the teaching beliefs and practices of university academics. *Review of Educational Research, 72*(2), 177–228.

Katzen, J. (2009, February/March). Technology brings challenges and opportunities for information. *Research Information*. Retrieved from https://www.researchinformation.info/feature/technology-brings-challenges-and-opportunities-information

Keig, L. (2000). Formative peer review of teaching: Attitudes of faculty at liberal arts colleges toward colleague assessment. *Journal of Personnel Evaluation in Education, 14*(1), 67–87.

Kezar, A. J. (2012). *Embracing non-tenure track faculty: Changing campuses for the new faculty majority*. New York, NY: Routledge.

Kezar, A., & Lester, J. (2009). Supporting faculty grassroots leadership. *Research in Higher Education, 50*(7), 715–740.

Kezar, A., & Maxey, D. (2012). *The changing faculty and student success: National trends for faculty composition over time*. Los Angeles, CA: University of Southern California, Pullias Center for Higher Education.

Kezar, A., & Maxey, D. (2016). *Envisioning the faculty for the twenty-first century*. New Brunswick, NJ: Rutgers University Press.

Kezar, A., & Sam, C. (2010). Special issue: Understanding the new majority of on-tenure-track faculty in higher education—Demographics, experiences, and plans of action. [*ASHE Higher Education Report, 36*(4)]. San Francisco, CA: Jossey-Bass.

Kiley, K. (2012a, November 19). Making the case. *Inside Higher Education*. Retrieved from https://www.insidehighered.com/news/2012/11/19/liberal-arts-colleges-rethink-their-messaging-face-criticism

Kiley, K. (2012b, October 12). New report on challenges facing research universities. *Inside Higher Ed*. Retrieved from https://www.insidehighered.com/quicktakes/2012/06/29/new-report-challenges-facing-research-universities

Kozeracki, C. A. (2002). Faculty attitudes about students. In C. L. Outcalt (Ed.), *New Directions for Community Colleges: No. 118. Community college faculty: Characteristics, practices, and challenges* (pp. 47–58). San Francisco, CA: Jossey-Bass.

Kreber, C. (2009). Supporting student learning in the context of diversity, complexity and uncertainty. In C. Kreber (Ed.), *The university and its disciplines: Teaching and learning within and beyond disciplinary boundaries* (pp. 3–18). New York, NY: Routledge.

Kuh, G. D. (2008). *Excerpt from "High-impact educational practices: What they are, who has access to them, and why they matter."* Washington, DC: Association of American Colleges and Universities.

Kuh, G. D., & Hu, S. (2001). The effects of student-faculty interaction in the 1990s. *The Review of Higher Education, 24*(3), 309–332.

Lane, A. (2013, June 2). Liberal arts colleges add degrees, sports, incentives to contend in highly competitive market. *Crain's Detroit Business*. Retrieved From http://www.crainsdetroit.com/article/20130602/NEWS/130609994/liberal-arts-colleges-add-degrees-sports-incentives-to-contend-in

Lattuca, L. R. (2001). *Creating interdisciplinarity: Interdisciplinary research and teaching among college and university faculty*. Nashville, TN: Vanderbilt University Press.

Lattuca, L. R., & Creamer, E. G. (2005). Learning as professional practice. In E. G. Creamer & L. R. Lattuca (Eds.), *New Directions for Teaching and Learning: No. 102. Advancing faculty learning through interdisciplinary collaboration* (pp. 3–11). San Francisco, CA: Jossey-Bass.

Lee, Y. S. (2000). The sustainability of university-industry research collaboration: An empirical assessment. *Journal of Technology Transfer, 25*(2), 111–133.

Levin, J. S. (2000). The revised institution: The community college mission at the end of the twentieth century. *Community College Review, 28*(2), 1–25.

Levin, J. S. (2004). The community college as a baccalaureate-granting institution. *Review of Higher Education, 28*(1), 1–22.

Levin, J. S. (2007). *Nontraditional students and community colleges: The conflict of justice and neoliberalism*. New York, NY: Palgrave and MacMillan.

Levin, J., Kater, S., & Wagoner, R. L. (2006). *Community college faculty: At work in the new economy*. New York, NY: Palgrave McMillan.

Lieberman, D. (2005). Beyond faculty development: How centers for teaching and learning can be laboratories for learning. In A. Kezar (Ed.), *New Directions for Higher Education: No. 131. Organizational learning in higher education* (pp. 87–98). San Francisco, CA: Jossey-Bass.

Lindholm, J. A. (2003). Perceived organizational fit: Nurturing the minds, hearts and personal ambitions of university faculty. *Review of Higher Education, 27*(1), 125–149.

Longanecker, D. A. (2008, November). *Mission differentiation vs. mission creep: Higher education's battle between creationism and evolution*. Retrieved from http://www.wiche.edu/info/gwypf/dal_mission.pdf

Love, J. (2008). Meeting the challenges of integrative learning: The Nexia concept. In D. R. Robertson & L. B. Nilson (Eds.), *To improve the academy: Vol. 26. Resources for faculty, instructional, and organizational development* (pp. 263–274). San Francisco, CA: Jossey-Bass.

Lowe, J. S. (2008). A participatory planning approach to enhancing a historically black university-community partnership: The case of the e-City initiative. *Planning, Practice & Research, 23*(4), 549–558.

Malcolm, L. E. (2013). Student diversity in community colleges: Examining trends and understanding the challenges. In J. S. Levin & S. T. Kater (Eds.), *Understanding community colleges* (pp. 19–36). New York, NY: Taylor & Francis.

Marshall I., Jr., Smith, B. D., Green, M. T., Anderson, B., Harry, S. V., Byrd, Y. M., … Hill, S. (2016). Scholarly productivity of social work faculty at historically Black colleges and universities: Are h-Index scores a suitable measure? *Journal of Social Work Education, 52*(1), 95–107.

Martinez, E. (2012). *Exploring faculty work expectations in light of the community college baccalaureate*. Paper presented at the Association for the Study of Higher Education Conference, Las Vegas, Nevada.

Martinez, E. (2014). *Growing pains: Exploring the transition from a community college into a four-year comprehensive college* (Doctoral dissertation). Retrieved from All Dissertations. (Paper 1342)

McArthur, R. C. (2005). Faculty-based advising: An important factor in community college retention. *Community College Review, 32*(1), 1–18.

McKinney, K. (2006). Attitudinal and structural factors contributing to challenges in the work of the scholarship of teaching and learning. In J. M. Braxton (Ed.), *New Directions for Institutional Research: No. 129. Analyzing faculty work and rewards: Using Boyer's four domains of scholarship,* (pp. 37–50). San Francisco, CA: Jossey-Bass.

McKinney, L., & Morris, P. A. (2010). Examining an evolution: A case study of organizational change accompanying the community college baccalaureate. *Community College Review, 37*(3), 187–208.

McKinney, L., Scicchitano, M., & Johns, T. (2013). A national survey of community college baccalaureate institutions. *Community College Journal of Research and Practice, 37*(1), 54–63.

Melguizo, T., & Strober, M. H. (2007). Faculty salaries and the maximization of prestige. *Research in Higher Education, 48*(6), 633–668.

Meier, K. (2013). Community college mission in historical perspective. In J. S. Levin & S. T. Kater (Eds.), *Understanding community colleges* (pp. 3–18). New York, NY: Taylor & Francis.

Milem, J. F., Berger, J. B., & Dey, E. L. (2000). Faculty time allocation: A study of change over twenty years. *Journal of Higher Education, 71*(4), 454–475.

Miller, E. R., & Skinner, R. A. (2012, May 7). Passionate traditionalist or pragmatic visionary? *Inside Higher Ed*. Retrieved from https://www.insidehighered.com/advice/2012/03/07/essay-next-generation-liberal-arts-college-presidents

Mohrman, K., Ma, W., & Baker, D. (2008). The research university in transition: The emerging global model. *Higher Education Policy*, *21*(1), 5–27.

Mooney, K. M., Fordham, T., & Lehr, V. (2005). A faculty development program to promote engaged classroom dialogue: The oral communication institute. In S. Chadwick-Blossey & D. R. Robertson (Eds.), *To improve the academy: Vol. 23. Resources for faculty, instructional, and organizational development* (pp. 219–235). Bolton, MA: Anker.

Morest, V. S. (2015). Faculty scholarship at community colleges: culture, institutional structures, and socialization. In J. M. Braxton (Ed.), *New Directions for Community Colleges: No. 171). Community college faculty scholarship* (pp. 21–36). San Francisco, CA: Jossey-Bass.

Morphew, C. C. (2002). "A rose by any other name": Which colleges become universities. *Review of Higher Education*, *25*, 207–223.

Morphew, C. C. (2009). Conceptualizing change in the institutional diversity of US colleges and universities. *Journal of Higher Education*, *80*(3), 243–269.

Murray, J. P. (2000). Faculty development in Texas two-year colleges. *Community College Journal of Research & Practice*, *24*(4), 251–267.

Murray, J. P. (2001). Faculty development in publicly supported 2-year colleges. *Community College Journal of Research and Practice*, *25*, 487–502.

Murray, J. P. (2002). The current state of faculty development in two-year colleges. In C. L. Outcalt (Ed.), *New Directions for Community Colleges: No. 118). Community college faculty: Characteristics, practices, and challenges* (pp. 89–98).). San Francisco, CA: Jossey-Bass.

National Center for Education Statistics. (2003). *Full-time and part-time faculty and institutional staff in degree-granting institutions, by type and control of institution and selected characteristics: Fall 1992, fall 1998, and fall 2003* (Table 252). Washington, DC: U.S. Department of Education.

National Center for Education Statistics. (2007). Total number of degree-granting institutions and fall enrollment in those institutions by type and control of institution and percentage of enrollment: 2007 (Table 230).

National Research Council. (2012). *Research universities and the future of America: Ten breakthrough actions vital to our nation's prosperity and security.* Washington, DC: National Academy of Science.

Nelson, W. C. (1981). *Renewal of the teacher scholar.* Washington, DC: Association of American Colleges.

Nelson, C. (2010, October 30). Parents, your children need professors with tenure. *The Chronicle of Higher Education.* Retrieved from http://www.chronicle.com/article/Parents-Your-Children-Need/124776/

Neumann, A. (2005a). Observations: Taking seriously the topic of learning in studies of faculty work and careers. In E. G. Creamer & L. Lattuca (Eds.), *New Directions for Teaching and Learning: No. 102. Advancing faculty learning through interdisciplinary collaboration* (pp. 63–83). San Francisco, CA: Jossey-Bass.

Neumann, A. (2005b). To glimpse beauty and awaken meaning: Scholarly learning as aesthetic experience. *Journal of Aesthetic Education*, *39*(2), 68–88.

Neumann, A. (2009a). *Professing to learn: Creating tenured lives and careers in the American research university.* Baltimore, MD: Johns Hopkins University Press.

Neumann, A. (2009b). Protecting the passion of scholars in times of change. *Change: The Magazine of Higher Learning*, *41*(2), 10–15.

Neumann, A. (2014). Staking a claim on learning: What we should know about learning in higher education, and why. *Review of Higher Education, 37*(2), 249–267.

Neumann, A., & Terosky, A. L. (2007). To give and to receive: Recently tenured professors' experiences of service in major research universities. *Journal of Higher Education, 78*(3), 282–310.

Neumann, A., Terosky, A. L., & Schell, J. (2006). Agents of learning: Strategies for assuming agency, for learning, in tenured faculty careers. In S. Bracken, J. K. Allen, & D. R. Dean (Eds.), *The balancing act: Gendered perspectives in faculty roles and work lives* (pp. 91–120). Sterling, VA: Stylus Publishing.

Nevarez, C., & Wood, J. L. (2010). *Community college leadership and administration: Theory, practice, and change* (Vol. 3). Oxford, UK: Peter Lang.

O'Meara, K. (2002). Uncovering the values in faculty evaluation of service as scholarship. *Review of Higher Education, 26*(1), 57–80.

O'Meara, K. A. (2005a). Effects of encouraging multiple forms of scholarship nationwide and across institutional types. In K. A. O'Meara & R. E. Rice (Eds.), *Faculty priorities reconsidered: Encouraging multiple forms of scholarship* (pp. 255–289). San Francisco, CA: Jossey-Bass.

O'Meara, K. A. (2005b). Encouraging multiple forms of scholarship in faculty reward systems: Does it make a difference? *Research in Higher Education, 46*(5), 479–510.

O'Meara, K. A. (2005c). Principles of good practice: Encouraging multiple forms of scholarship in policy and practice. In K. A. O'Meara & R. E. Rice (Eds.), *Faculty priorities reconsidered: Encouraging multiple forms of scholarship* (pp. 290–302). San Francisco, CA: Jossey-Bass.

O'Meara, K.A. (2006). Encouraging multiple forms of scholarship in faculty reward systems: Have academic cultures really changed? In J. Braxton (Ed.), *New Directions for Institutional Research: No. 129. Analyzing faculty work and rewards: Using Boyer's four domains of scholarship* (pp. 77–96). San Francisco, CA: Jossey-Bass.

O'Meara, K. A. (2007). Striving for what? Exploring the pursuit of prestige. In J. D. Smart (Ed.), *Higher education: Handbook of theory and research, 22* (pp. 121–179). New York, NY: Springer.

O'Meara, K. (2011). Inside the panopticon: Studying academic reward systems. In J. C. Smart & M. B. Paulsen (Eds.), *Higher education: Handbook of theory and research, 26* (pp. 161–220). New York, NY: Springer.

O'Meara, K. (2015). *Flexible workplace agreements: Enabling higher education's strategic advantage.* New York, NY: TIAA-CREF Institute. Retrieved from https://www.tiaainstitute.org/public/pdf/flexible_workplace_agreements.pdf

O'Meara, K., & Rice, R. E. (2005). *Faculty priorities reconsidered: Rewarding multiple forms of scholarship.* San Francisco, CA: Jossey-Bass.

O'Meara, K., Terosky, A. L., and Neumann, A. (2008). Faculty careers and work lives: A professional growth perspective. [*ASHE Higher Education Report, 34(3)*]. San Francisco, CA: Jossey-Bass.

Ortquist-Ahrens, L., & Weispfenning, J. (2007). Faculty development at a small College: Giving wing to faculty visions for excellence in teaching and learning. In *Proceedings of the NCA Higher Learning Commission 2007 Annual Meeting: Leading for the Common Good: Leading the College or University* (pp.122–127).

Outcalt, C. (2002). *A profile of the community college professoriate, 1975–2000.* New York, NY: Routledge.

Padovan, P., & Whittington, D. (1998). Rewarding faculty scholarship at two-year colleges: Incentive for change or perceived threat. *Community College Journal of Research and Practice, 22*(3), 213–228.

Palmer, J. C. (1992). The scholarly activities of community college faculty. In J. C. Palmer & G. B. Vaughan (Eds.), *Fostering a climate for faculty scholarship at community colleges* (pp. 49–65). Washington, DC: American Association of Community and Junior Colleges. Retrieved from http://files.eric.ed.gov/fulltext/ED350048.pdf

Palmer, J. C. (2015). Scholarship and the professional identity of community college faculty members. In J. M. Braxton (Ed.), *New Directions for Community Colleges: No. 171. Community college faculty scholarship* (pp. 37–48). San Francisco, CA: Jossey-Bass.

Park, T. J., & Braxton, J. M. (2013). Delineating scholarly types of college and university faculty members. *Journal of Higher Education, 84*(3), 301–328.

Park, T. J., Braxton, J. M., & Lyken-Segosebe, D. (2015). Types of faculty scholars in community college. In J. M. Braxton (Ed.), *New Directions for Community Colleges: No. 171. Community college faculty scholarship* (pp. 15–19). San Francisco, CA: Jossey-Bass.

Pascarella, E. T., Cruce, T. M., Wolniak, G. C., & Blaich, C. F. (2004). Do liberal arts colleges really foster good practices in undergraduate education? *Journal of College Student Development, 45*(1), 57–74.

Perez, J. A. (2003). Undergraduate research at two-year colleges. In J. Kinkead (Ed.), *New Directions for Teaching and Learning: No. 93. Valuing and supporting undergraduate research* (pp. 69–77). San Francisco, CA: Jossey-Bass.

Perniciaro, R. C., Nespoli, L. A., & Anbarasan, S. (2015). Filling the void: The roles of a local applied research center and a statewide workforce training consortium. In J. M. Braxton (Ed.), *New Directions for Community Colleges: No. 171. Community college faculty scholarship* (pp. 63–75). San Francisco, CA: Jossey-Bass.

Persellin, D., & Goodrick, T. (2012). Faculty development in higher education: Long-term impact of a summer teaching and learning workshop. *Journal of the Scholarship of Teaching and Learning, 10*(1), 1–13.

Peters, D., Schodt, D., & Walczak, M. (2008). Supporting the scholarship of teaching and learning at liberal arts colleges. In D. R. Robertson & L.B. Nilson (Eds.), *To improve the academy: Vol. 26. Resources for faculty, instructional, and organizational development* (pp. 68–84). San Francisco, CA: Jossey-Bass.

Piaget, J. (1975). *The development of thought: Equilibration of cognitive structures.* New York, NY: Viking.

Prager, C. (2003). Scholarship matters. *Community College Journal of Research and Practice, 27*, 579–592.

Provasnik, S., & Planty, M. (2008). *Community colleges: Special supplement to the condition of education 2008* (NCES 2008–033). Washington, DC: National Center for Education Statistics. Retrieved from http://nces.ed.gov/pubs2008/2008033.pdf

Rawlings, H. R. (2012, March 30). Why research universities must change. *Inside Higher Ed.* Retrieved from https://www.insidehighered.com/views/2012/03/30/essay-research-universities-must-pay-more-attention-student-learning

Quijada Cerecer, P. D., Ek, L. D., Alanis, I., & Murakami-Ramalho, E. (2011). Transformative resistance as agency: Chicanas/Latinas (re)creating academic spaces. *Journal of the Professoriate, 5*(1), 70–98.

Reder, M. (2007). Does your college really support teaching and learning? *Peer Review 9*(4), 9–13.

Reder, M., Mooney, K., Holmgren, R. A., & Kuerbis, P. J. (2009). Starting and sustaining successful faculty development programs at small colleges. *To Improve the Academy, 27*, 267–286.

Reindl, T., & Brower, D. (2001). Financing state colleges and universities: What is happening to the "public" in public higher education? *College and University, 77*(1), 29.

Reichman, H. (2015). Does academic freedom have a future? *Academe, 101*(6), 1–6.

Research Universities Futures Consortium (2012, June). *The current health and future well-being of the American research university.* Retrieved from https://www.elsevier.com/__data/assets/pdf_file/0004/53185/Research-Universities-Futures-Consortium.pdf

Rhoades, G. (1998). *Managed professionals: Unionized faculty and restructuring academic labor.* Albany, NY: State University of New York.

Rhoades, G. (2007). The study of the academic profession. In P. J. Gumport (Ed.), *Sociology of higher education: Contributions and their contexts* (pp. 113–146). Baltimore, MD: Johns Hopkins University Press.

Rhoten, D. 2010. Interdisciplinary research: Trend or transition? *Insights from the Social Sciences.* Retrieved from http://items.ssrc.org/interdisciplinary-research-trend-or-transition/

Rice, R. E., & Sorcinelli, M. D. (2002). Can the tenure process be improved? In R. Chait (Ed.), *The questions of tenure* (pp. 101–124). Cambridge, MA: Harvard University Press.

Richlin, L., & Cox, M. D. 2004. Developing scholarly teaching and the scholarship of teaching and learning through faculty learning communities. In M. D. Cox & L. Richlin (Eds.), *New Directions for Teaching and Learning: No. 97. Building faculty learning communities* (pp. 127–136). San Francisco, CA: Jossey-Bass.

Robison, S. (2013). *The peak performing professor: A practical guide to productivity and happiness.* San Francisco, CA: Jossey-Bass.

Rosser, V. J. (2004). Faculty members' intentions to leave: A national study on their worklife and satisfaction. *Research in Higher Education, 45*(3), 285–309.

Rowell, K. (2010). The community college conundrum: pitfalls and possibilities of professional sociological associations. *Sociological Focus, 43*(3), 167–184.

Russell, A. (2010, October). *Update on the community college baccalaureate: Evolving trends and issues.* Washington, DC: American Association of State Colleges and Universities. Retrieved from http://www.aascu.org/uploadedFiles/AASCU/Content/Root/PolicyAndAdvocacy/PolicyPublications/AASCU_Update_Community_College_Baccalaureate(1).pdf

Ryan, J. F., Healy, R., & Sullivan, J. (2012). Oh, won't you stay? Predictors of faculty intent to leave a public research university. *Higher Education, 63*(4), 421–437.

Sá, C. M. (2008). "Interdisciplinary strategies" in US research universities. *Higher Education, 55*(5), 537–552.

Schroeder, C. (2012). *Coming in from the margins: Faculty development's emerging organizational development role in institutional change.* Sterling, VA: Stylus Publishing.

Schuster, J. H., & Finkelstein, M. J. (2006). *The American faculty: The restructuring of academic work and careers.* Baltimore, MD: Johns Hopkins University Press.

Shulman, L. (2004a). *Teaching as community property: Essays on higher education.* San Francisco, CA: Jossey-Bass.

Shulman, L. (2004b). *The wisdom of practice: Essays on learning, teaching, and learning to teach.* San Francisco, CA: Jossey-Bass.

Shulman, L. S., & Hutchings, P. (1998). *About the scholarship of teaching and learning: The Pew scholars national fellowship program.* Menlo Park, CA: Carnegie Foundation for the Advancement of Teaching.

Selingo, J. (2000, November 17). Facing new missions and rivals, state colleges seek a makeover: Can the undistinguished middle child of public higher education find a fresh identity? *Chronicle of Higher Education*, pp. 40–42.

Slaughter, S., & Rhoades, G. (2004). *Academic capitalism.* Baltimore, MD: Johns Hopkins University Press.

Snyder, T. S., de Brey, C., & Dillow, S. A. (2016a). *Digest of education statistics, 2014.* Washington, DC: National Center for Education Statistics, U.S. Department of Education. Retrieved from https://nces.ed.gov/pubs2016/2016006.pdf

Snyder, T. S., de Brey, C., & Dillow, S. A. (2016b). *Digest of education statistics, 2015.* Washington, DC: National Center for Education Statistics, U.S. Department of Education. Retrieved from https://nces.ed.gov/pubs2016/2016014.pdf

Soo, D. (2011). Envisioning a regional role: Comprehensive universities and conceptions of their regional contributions (Doctoral dissertation). Retrieved from University of Pennsylvania. Publicly Accessible Penn Dissertations. (Paper 583)

Sorcinelli, M. D. (2002). New conceptions of scholarship for a new generation of faculty members. In K. J. Zahorski (Ed.), *New Directions for Teaching and Learning: No. 90. Scholarship in the postmodern era: New venues, new values, new visions* (pp. 41–48). San Francisco, CA: Jossey-Bass

Sorcinelli, M. D. (2007). Faculty development: The challenge going forward. *Peer Review, 9*(4).

Sorcinelli, M. D., Austin, A. E., Eddy, P. L., & Beach, A. L. (2005). *Creating the future of faculty development: Learning from the past, understanding the present.* Bolton, MA: Anker.

Sperling, C. B. (2003). How community colleges understand the scholarship of teaching and learning. *Community College Journal of Research and Practice, 27*, 593–601.

Sullivan, W. M. (1995). *Work and integrity: The crisis and promise of professionalism in America.* New York, NY: Harper Business.

Sydnor, K. D., Hawkins, A. S., & Edwards, L. V. (2010). Expanding research opportunities: Making the argument for the fit between HBCUs and community-based participatory research. *Journal of Negro Education, 79*(1), 79–86.

Tang, T. L., & Chamberlain, M. (2003). Effects of rank, tenure, length of service, and institution on faulty attitudes toward research and teaching: The case of regional state universities. *Journal of Education for Business, 79*(2), 103–110.

Terosky, A. L. (2005). *Taking teaching seriously: A study of university professors and their undergraduate teaching* (Unpublished doctoral dissertation). New York, NY: Teachers College Columbia University.

Terosky, A. L., & Gonzales, L. (2015). Re-envisioned contributions: Experiences of faculty employed at institutional types that differ from their original aspirations. *Review of Higher Education, 39*(2), 241–268.

Terosky, A. L. & Gonzales, L. (2016). Scholarly learning as vocation: A study of community and broad access liberal arts college faculty. *Innovative Higher Education, 41*(2), 105–120.

Terosky, A., Phifer, T., & Neumann, A. (2008). Shattering plexiglass: Continuing challenges for women professors in research universities. In J. Glazer-Raymo (Ed.), *Unfinished agendas:*

New and continuing gender challenges in higher education (pp. 52–79). Baltimore, MD: Johns Hopkins University Press.

Thelin, J. R. (2004). *A history of American higher education.* Baltimore, MD: Johns Hopkins University Press.

Thelin, J. R. (2011). *A history of American higher education* (2nd ed.). Baltimore, MD: Johns Hopkins University Press.

Tierney, W. G., & Bensimon, E. M. (1996). *Promotion and tenure: Community and socialization in academe.* Albany, NY: SUNY Press.

Tinberg, H. B. (1997). *Border talk: Writing and knowing in the two-year college.* Urbana, IL: National Council of Teachers of English.

Tinberg, H., Duffy, D. K., & Mino, J. (2007). The scholarship of teaching and learning at the two-year college: Promise and peril. *Change: The Magazine of Higher Learning, 39*(4), 26–33.

Toma, J. D. (2012). Institutional strategy: Positioning for prestige. In M. N. Bastedo (Ed.), *The organization of higher education: Managing colleges for a new era* (pp. 118–159). Baltimore, MD: Johns Hopkins University Press.

Toth, C. (2014). Unmeasured engagement: Two-year college English faculty and disciplinary professional organizations. *Teaching English in the Two-Year College, 41*(4), 335.

Toutkoushian, R. K., Porter, S. R., Danielson, C., & Hollis, P. R. (2003). Using publications counts to measure an institution's research productivity. *Research in Higher Education, 44,* 121–148.

Townsend, B. K., & Twombly, S. B. (2007). *Community college faculty: Overlooked and under-valued.* [*ASHE Higher Education Report, 32(6)*]. San Francisco, CA: Jossey-Bass.

Trow, M. (2001). From mass higher education to universal access: The American advantage. In P. G. Altbach, P. J. Gumport, & D. B. Johnstone (Eds.), *In defense of American higher education* (pp. 110–143). Baltimore, MD: Johns Hopkins University Press.

Trower, C. A. (2012). *Success on the tenure track: Five keys to faculty job satisfaction.* Baltimore, MD: Johns Hopkins University Press.

Twombly, S., & Townsend, B. K. (2008). Community college faculty: What we know and need to know. *Community College Review, 36*(1), 5–24.

U.S. Department of Education. (2015). *IPEDS institutional comparisons.* Washington, DC: Author.

U.S. Department of Education. (2008). *IPEDS institutional comparisons.* Washington, DC: Author.

Umbach, P. D., & Kuh, G. D. (2006). Student experiences with diversity at liberal arts colleges: Another claim for distinctiveness. *Journal of Higher Education, 77*(1), 169–192.

Van Rijnsoever, F. J., & Hessels, L. K. (2011). Factors associated with disciplinary and inter-disciplinary research collaboration. *Research Policy, 40*(3), 463–472.

Vaughan, G. B. (1988). Scholarship in community colleges: The path to respect. *Educational Record, 69*(2), 26–31.

Vaughan, G. B. (2006). *The community college story* (3rd ed.). Washington, DC: Community College Press.

Vitullo, M. W., & Spalter-Roth, R. (2013). Contests for professional status community college faculty in sociology. *American Sociologist, 44,* 349–365.

Walker, J. D., Baepler, P., & Cohen, B. (2008). The scholarship of teaching and learning paradox: Results without rewards. *College Teaching, 56*(3), 183–189.

Walker, K. P. (2005). History, rationale, and the community college baccalaureate association. In D. L. Floyd, M. L. Skolnik, & K. P. Walker (Eds.), *The community college baccalaureate: Emerging trends & policy issues* (pp. 9–23). Sterling, VA: Stylus Publishing.

Ward, K. (2003). Faculty service roles and the rice of scholarship of engagement. [*ASHE-ERIC Higher Education Report, 29*(5)]. San Francisco, CA: Jossey-Bass.

Ward, K., & Wolf-Wendel, L. E. (2005). Work and family perspectives from research university faculty. In J. W. Curtis (Ed.), *New Directions for Higher Education: No. 130. The challenge of balancing faculty careers and family work* (pp. 67–80). San Francisco, CA: Jossey-Bass.

White House. (2010, October 5). Background on the White House summit on community colleges. Retrieved from https://www.whitehouse.gov/the-press-office/2010/10/05/background-white-house-summit-community-colleges

White House. (2014, July 22). Fact sheet: Ready to work at a glance: Job-driven training and American opportunity. Retrieved from https://www.whitehouse.gov/the-press-office/2014/07/22/fact-sheet-ready-work-glance-job-driven-training-and-american-opportunit

Wolf-Wendel, L. E., & Ward, K. (2006). Faculty life at comprehensive colleges and universities: The perspective of women faculty. *Journal of the Professoriate, 1*, 5–21.

Wolf-Wendel, L. E., Ward, K., & Twombly, S. B. (2007). Faculty life at community colleges: The perspective of women with children. *Community College Review, 34*(4), 255–281.

Wood, J. L., & Nevarez, C. (2014). *Ethical leadership and the community college: Paradigms, decision-making, and praxis*. Charlotteb, NC: Information Age Publishing.

Wright, M. C., Assar, N., Kain, E. L., Kramer, L., Howery, C. B., McKinney, K., ... Atkinson, M. (2004). Greedy institutions: The importance of institutional context for teaching in higher education. *Teaching Sociology, 32*(2): 144–159.

Wright, M. (2005). Always at odds?: Congruence in faculty beliefs about teaching at a research university. *Journal of Higher Education, 76*(3), 331–353.

Wright, R. E. (2006). Student evaluations of faculty: Concerns raised in the literature, and possible solutions. *College Student Journal, 40*(2), 417.

Youn, T. I. K., & Price, T. M. (2009). Learning from the experience of others: The evolution of faculty tenure and promotion rules in comprehensive institutions. *Journal of Higher Education, 80*, 204–237.

Zusman, A. (2005). Challenges facing higher education in the twenty-first century. In P. G. Altbach, R. O. Berdahl, P. J. Gumport (Eds.), *American higher education in the twenty-first century: Social, political, and economic challenges* (2nd ed., pp. 115–160). Baltimore, MD: Johns Hopkins University Press.

Name Index

A

Abbott, A., 45
Acevedo-Gil, N., 93
Àkerlind, G. S., 47
Alanis, I., 110
Albert, M., 116
Altbach, P. G., 31
Ambler, M., 96, 110
Amey, M. J., 92
Anbarasan, S., 99
Anderson, B., 43
Andrews, M. L., 41
Aper, J., 65
Archibald, T., 105
Arreola, R. A., 17
Assar, N., 64
Atkinson, M., 64
Austin, A. E., 18, 19, 26, 29, 92, 119
Ayers, D. F., 91

B

Baepler, P., 65
Baez, B., 89
Bailey, T., 93
Bailey, T. R., 93
Baker, D., 35
Baker, V. L., 19, 49, 71, 72, 73, 74, 75, 76,
    77, 81, 82, 83, 84, 85, 86, 112
Baldwin, R. G., 71, 76, 83, 86
Bardo, J. W., 54
Beach, A. L., 18, 19

Becker, W. E., 41
Bemmel, E. P., 94
Bensimon, E. M., 50, 118
Bentley, P. J., 34
Berger, J. B., 33, 34
Beversluis, C. D., 80
Blackburn, R. T., 19
Blaich, C. F., 78
Bloomgarden, A. H., 118
Bogue, E. G., 65
Bowen, W., 35, 36
Boyer, E. L., 9, 10, 11, 13, 15, 17, 18, 20,
    21, 22, 23, 27, 28, 29, 30, 31, 38, 40,
    42, 44, 45, 49, 52, 58, 59, 60, 61, 63,
    65, 66, 67, 68, 70, 77, 79, 80, 82, 83,
    84, 86, 95, 96, 98, 100, 102, 103, 105,
    108, 109, 110, 112, 115, 116, 117, 119
Bozeman, B., 27, 38
Bradburn, E. M., 91
Brawer, F. B., 89, 95
Braxton, J. M., 18, 29, 58, 60, 61, 62, 63,
    65, 90, 91, 92, 94, 95, 98, 99, 100, 101,
    102, 103, 104, 105, 108, 109, 113, 116,
    117
Breneman, D. W., 71, 75, 76
Brint, S., 18, 35
Brower, D., 35
Brown, G. A., 16
Bryan, V. C., 94
Buchanan, H. E., 61
Buckley, J., 105

Buller, J., 19
Bull, J., 16
Byrd, Y. M., 43
Byrne, S., 45, 113, 116

C

Campbell, C. M., 109
Campbell, L. M., 116
Cantwell, B., 48
Cariaga-Lo, L., 18
Cataldi, E. F., 91
Cejda, B. D., 93, 95, 96, 101, 102, 104, 108
Chamberlain, M., 54
Chang, M. J., 49
Chism, N. V., 78
Chopp, R., 70
Clark, B. R., 13, 20, 75, 118
Cohen, A. M., 89, 90, 91, 92, 93, 95, 101
Cohen, B., 65
Colbeck, C. L., 67
Cole, J. R., 31
Conrad, C., 89
Conrad, C. F., 110
Cooke, N. J., 46
Coser, L. A., 64
Cox, M. D., 67
Crazy Bull, C., 110
Creamer, E. G., 24, 46, 50, 114
Cruce, T. M., 78
Cruz, L., 65, 66, 113
Cuellar, M., 93
Curry, J. M., 80

D

Danielson, C., 60
D'Avanzo, C., 78
Dawkins, P. W., 18
de Brey, C., 88
Delgado-Bernal, D., 117
Dewey, J., 24
Dey, E. L., 33, 34
Diamond, N., 31
Diamond, R. M., 29
Dillow, S. A., 88

Doran, E., 114
Dougherty, K. J., 26, 55, 94, 119
Duffy, D. K., 93, 97
Duran, J. L., 46

E

Eagan, K., 91
Eagan, M. K., Jr., 49
Eddy, P. L., 18, 19, 93
Edwards, L. V., 43
Ehrenberg, R. G., 18, 115
Ek, L. D., 110
Ellern, G. D., 65, 66, 113
Enger, R., 18
Entwistle, N., 16
Etzkowitz, H., 33
Evenbeck, S., 78

F

Fahimi, M., 91
Fain, P., 94
Fairweather, J. S., 40, 42, 47, 113, 116
Fayne, H. R., 78
Ferrall, V. E., Jr., 71
Finkelstein, M. J., 18, 26, 33, 36, 55, 91, 92, 114, 115, 119
Fink, J., 93
Floyd, D. L., 90, 94
Ford, G., 65, 66, 113
Fordham, T., 78
Formicola, A., 45
Freire, P., 24
Frost, S., 70
Frost, S. H., 41, 42
Fugate, A. L., 92

G

Gandara, P., 93
Gappa, J. M., 19, 26, 107
Gardner, S. K., 90, 112, 114, 119
Gasman, M., 89, 110
Gaughan, M., 27, 38
Geiger, R. L., 54
Gillespie, K., 19
Givens, T. E., 9, 16
Glassick, C. E., 29, 117

Goldrick-Rab, S., 93
Gonzales, L., 11, 16, 20, 22, 25, 29, 39, 56, 58, 59, 61, 64, 65, 67, 77, 81, 84, 85, 86, 94–99, 102, 104, 105, 108, 109, 110, 113, 114, 117
Gonzales, L. D., 24, 26, 38, 39, 91, 112, 113, 114, 116, 117
Goodrick, T., 79
Gorman, J. C., 46
Gornall, L., 64, 67
Graham, H. D., 31
Green, M. T., 43
Greer, J., 49
Grubb, W. N., 54, 55
Gulbrandsen, M., 46
Gumport, P. J., 31

H

Hagedorn, L. S., 93, 97, 98, 103, 117
Hansen, D. T., 58, 59, 69
Hargraves, M., 105
Harry, S. V., 43
Harvey, D., 108
Hawkins, A. S., 43
Healy, R., 38
Heath, C., 40
Heffner, G. G., 80
Helland, P., 29
Helland, P. A., 29, 61
Henderson, B. B., 18, 20, 39, 54–57, 59, 60, 61, 62, 63, 65, 66, 108, 114, 115, 116
Hensel, N., 93, 95, 96, 101, 102, 108
Hensel, N. H., 95, 96, 104
Hermanowicz, J. C., 24, 26, 108, 109, 115
Hessels, L. K., 46
Hill, S., 43
Holley, K., 45
Holley, K. A., 45
Hollis, P. R., 60
Holmgren, R. A., 78, 79
Hora, M. T., 116
Howery, C. B., 64
Huber, M., 17
Huber, M. T., 29, 65, 113

Hughes, A., 73
Hurtado, S., 49
Hu, S., 46, 49
Hutchings, P., 29, 65, 113

I

Ihas, D., 49

J

Jacobs, J. A., 45
Jaeger, A. J., 17
Jaggars, S. S., 93
Jenkins, D., 93
Jenkins, R., 92
Johnson, D. R., 18
Johnson, W. B., 49
Johns, T., 93
Johnstone, D. B., 31

K

Kain, E. L., 64
Kane, R., 40
Kane, W. D., 54, 60
Kater, S., 91
Katzen, J., 36
Kauppinen, I., 48
Keig, L., 78
Kezar, A., 16, 18, 19, 47, 48, 118
Kezar, A. J., 17, 118
Kiley, K., 35, 76
Kisker, C. B., 89
Kozeracki, C. A., 92
Kramer, L., 64
Kreber, C., 84
Kuerbis, P. J., 79
Kuh, G. D., 46, 49, 72, 101
Kyvik, S., 34, 35

L

Lane, A., 76
Lattuca, L. R., 24, 26, 45, 46
Lawrence, J. H., 19
Lazerson, M., 54, 55
Lees, N. D., 78
Lee, Y. S., 46
Lehr, V., 78

Lester, J., 47, 48
Levin, J., 91, 92
Levin, J. S., 90, 91, 93
Lieberman, D., 78
Lindholm, J. A., 26
Longanecker, D. A., 94
Love, J., 80, 81
Lowe, J. S., 43, 44
Luckey, W., 29
Luckey, W. T., 29, 61
Lunsford, L. G., 19, 49, 74, 83
Lyken-Segosebe, D., 98, 99, 100

M

Maeroff, G. I., 29
Makker, S., 71
Malcolm, L. E., 90
Marshall, I., Jr., 43
Martinez, E., 93, 95, 96, 102, 103, 104, 108, 114
Ma, W., 35
Maxey, D., 16, 18, 19
McArthur, R. C., 95
McDaniels, M., 29
McKinney, K., 61
McKinney, L., 93, 94, 103
Meier, K., 89
Melguizo, T., 38, 39
Milem, J. F., 33, 34
Miller, E. R., 70
Mino, J., 93
Mohrman, K., 35, 50
Mooney, K., 79
Mooney, K. M., 78
Morest, V. S., 103, 117, 118
Morphew, C. C., 59, 76
Morris, P. A., 103
Moser, D., 18
Mosqueda, C. M., 49
Moss, H., 65, 66, 113
Murakami-Ramalho, E., 110
Murray, J. P., 97, 113

N

Nelson, C., 16
Nelson, W. C., 75

Nespoli, L. A., 99
Neumann, A., 16, 17, 21–27, 37, 40, 50, 58, 59, 67, 107, 108, 109, 113, 115, 116, 118
Nevarez, C., 93
Núñez, A. M., 114

O

O'Meara, K., 15, 17, 18, 20, 29, 42, 44, 65, 66, 92, 108, 109, 113
O'Meara, K. A., 29, 42, 44, 57, 59, 60, 64, 65, 76, 108, 113, 114, 117, 118
Ortquist-Ahrens, L., 78
Outcalt, C., 91

P

Padovan, P., 97
Palmer, J. C., 102, 103, 112, 114
Park, T. J., 58, 63, 100, 108
Pascarella, E. T., 78
Pendlebury, M., 16
Perez, J. A., 95, 102, 103, 104
Perniciaro, R. C., 99
Persellin, D., 79
Peters, D., 78, 80, 83, 113
Phifer, T., 115
Piaget, J., 24
Pifer, M. J., 19, 49, 74, 83
Planty, M., 91, 92, 93, 101
Porter, S. R., 60
Prager, C., 101, 112
Price, T. M., 59
Provasnik, S., 91, 92, 93, 101

Q

Quijada Cerecer, P. D., 110

R

Ramsden, P., 16
Rawlings, H. R., 40
Ream, T. C., 18
Reder, M., 79
Reichman, H., 16
Reindl, T., 35

Rhoades, G., 21, 37, 48, 92
Rhoten, D., 113, 116
Rice, R. E., 18, 29, 65, 113
Richlin, L., 67
Rincones, R., 24, 26, 39, 113, 116
Rivard, J. K., 19
Robertson, D. L., 19
Robison, S., 19
Rosser, V. J., 38
Rowell, K., 108
Russell, A., 90, 93, 94
Ryan, J. F., 38, 39

S

Sá, C. M., 45
Salisbury, J., 64, 67
Salmi, J., 31
Sam, C., 19, 118
Sandretto, S., 40
Santos, R., 93
Schell, J., 26
Schodt, D., 78, 83
Schotter, A., 18
Schroeder, C., 19
Schuster, J. H., 18, 26, 33, 36, 55, 91, 92, 114, 115, 119
Scicchitano, M., 93
Selingo, J., 65
Sharkness, J., 49
Shulman, L., 67
Shulman, L. S., 29
Skinner, R. A., 70
Slaughter, S., 48
Smeby, J. C., 46
Smith, B. D., 43
Snyder, T. S., 88, 91
Solorzano, D., 93
Soo, D., 55, 62
Sorcinelli, M. D., 18, 19, 29, 78
Spalter-Roth, R., 108
Spence, C., 18
Sperling, C. B., 97, 98, 103
Strober, M. H., 38, 39
Sullivan, J., 38
Sullivan, W. M., 108
Sydnor, K. D., 43, 110

T

Tang, T. L., 54
Taylor, A. R., 46
Teodorescu, D., 41, 42
Terosky, A., 17
Terosky, A. L., 16, 20, 22, 25, 26, 29, 39, 42, 50, 56, 58, 59, 61, 64, 65, 67, 77, 81, 84, 85, 86, 94–99, 102, 104, 105, 108, 113, 115, 117
Thelin, J. R., 54, 71
Tierney, W. G., 50, 118
Tinberg, H, 93, 101, 102, 103, 112
Tinberg, H. B., 108, 112
Toma, J. D., 94
Toth, C., 102, 104, 108
Toutkoushian, R. K., 60
Townsend, B. K., 90, 91, 92, 94, 97, 101, 105, 112, 113
Trice, A. G., 19, 26
Trochim, W. M., 105
Trower, C. A., 19, 26
Trow, M., 33, 35, 36
Turner, C. S. V., 89
Twombly, S., 90, 91
Twombly, S. B., 90, 91, 92, 97, 101, 105, 112, 113

U

Umbach, P. D., 72

V

Van Rijnsoever, F. J., 46
Vaughan, G. B., 89, 91, 101, 112
Villalpando, O., 117
Vitullo, M. W., 108

W

Wagoner, R. L., 91
Walczak, M., 78, 83
Walker, J. D., 65, 67, 113
Walker, K. P., 90, 93, 94
Ward, K., 37, 50, 54, 66, 92
Weispfenning, J., 78
Weiss, D. H., 70
Wharton-Michael, P., 67
White, B., 65, 66, 113

Whittington, D., 97
Wolf-Wendel, L. E., 37, 54, 66, 92
Wolniak, G. C., 78
Wood, J. L., 93
Wright, M., 41, 42
Wright, M. C., 64
Wright, R. E., 17

Y
Youn, T. I. K., 59

Z
Zhang, L., 18, 115
Zimbler, L., 91
Zusman, A., 36

Subject Index

A

Academic capitalism, 48
Academic drift, 76
Academy for Global Engagement (AGE) Fellowship Program, 43
Achieving the Dream: Community Colleges Count, 97
A Guide to Faculty Development, 19
American Association of Community Colleges (AACC), 89
The American Community College, 89
American Council on Education, 34
Argosy University, 36
ASHE Higher Education, 17
Atlantic Cape Community College, 99

B

Baccalaureate Colleges, 53
Baccalaureate institutions, 71
Beacon Conference, 95
Boyer's forms, of scholarship, 27–30

C

Calvin College, 80
Carnegie Academy for the Scholarship of Teaching and Learning's (CASTL), 80
Carnegie Classification of Institutions of Higher Education, 32, 54
Carnegie Foundation for the Advancement of Teaching, 59

Center for Regional and Business Center, 99
Centers for teaching and learning (CTL), 78
Chief academic officers (CAO), 44
College of Agriculture and Natural Resources (CANR), 43
College of Engineering (CoE), 43
Community College of Baltimore County (CCBC), 98
Community colleges, 88–89; barriers to faculty scholarly learning at, 100–102; challenges, 93–94; defined, 89; faculty, 90–93; faculty scholarly learning, 94–100; implications of, 105–106; mission, 89–90; opportunities for faculty scholarly learning at, 103–104; students, 90
Community College Undergraduate Research Initiative (CCURI), 95
Comprehensive colleges and universities: challenges, 56–57; defined, 53–54; faculty, 55–56; mission, 54–55; students, 55
Consummatory scholarship, 63
Context, defined, 24
Council on Undergraduate Research (CUR), 95
The Current Health and Future Well-Being of the American Research University, 35

D

Department of Urban and Regional Planning (DURP), 43
Developing Faculty in Liberal Arts Colleges, 73
DeVry Institutes of Technology, 36

E

e-City Initiative, 43
Emerging Global Model, 50
Emory University, 41
Engagement, scholarship of, 42–45
Envisioning the Faculty for the Twenty-First Century: Moving to a Mission-Oriented and Learner-Centered Model, 19
Evaluative thinking (ET), 105; goal of, 106

F

Faculty Priorities Reconsidered, 18
Faculty scholarly learning, advancing the study of, 119–120; barriers, 111–115; findings and implications, 107–111; future directions, 118–119; opportunities, 115–118
Faculty scholarly learning, at comprehensives, 57–59, 63–64; barriers to, 64–66; implications of, 68–69; opportunities for, 66–67; scholarship of discovery, 59–60; scholarship of engagement, 62; scholarship of integration, 63; scholarship of teaching, 60–62
Faculty Survey of Student Engagement (FSSE), 33; in Research Universities, 34; time allocation, 56
Fannie Mae Foundation, 43
The forgotten colleges of America, 54

G

Geographic information systems (GIS), 99
Geological Society of America, 104
Great Lakes Colleges Association (GLCA), 73; hours on task across, 74
A Guide for Applying to Jobs at Selective Liberal Arts Colleges, 82

H

Higher Education Research Institute, 34, 119
Historically Black colleges and universities (HBCU), 43
Hyperprofessionality, 64

I

Immersed Scholars, 100
Indiana University, 73
Initiative for Faculty Development in Liberal Arts Colleges (IFDLAC), 74
Institute for Scientific Information Index, 60
Integration, scholarship of, 45–46

J

Jackson State University (JSU), 43
Johns Hopkins University, 31
Joy Shechtman Mankoff Center for Teaching & Learning, 79

L

Learning, defined, 23–24
Liberal Arts Colleges (LAC), 21, 70; barriers to faculty scholarly learning in, 81–84; challenges, 75–76; defined, 71; faculty, 72–75; faculty scholarly learning in, 76–81; FSSE time allocation, 73; implications of, 86–87; mission, 70–72; opportunities for scholarly learning in, 84–86; students, 72

M

Macomb Community College (MCC), 98
Michigan State University, 43
Minority serving institutions (MSI), 21
Mission confusion. *See* Striving institutions

N

National Center for Education Statistics (NCES), 32, 55, 56, 119
National Center for the Study of Collective Bargaining in Higher Education and the Professions, 92

National Council of Instructional
 Administrators (NCIA), 95
National Science Foundation, 102
National Study of Postsecondary Faculty
 (NSOPF), 92, 119
National Survey of Student Engagement,
 73
Navajo health problems, 96
New Century Scholars, 50
New Directions for Community Colleges, 94,
 109
*Non-Tenure Track Faculty in Higher
 Education: Theories and Tensions,* 19

P

People's Universities, 54

R

Research universities: barriers to scholarly
 learning in, 46–48; defined, 31–37;
 faculty scholarly learning in, 37–46;
 implications of, 51–52; opportunities
 for scholarly learning in, 49–51
Research Universities Futures Consortium,
 35, 37, 48
Rutgers University, 36

S

Scholarly learning, 16; in academic career,
 26–27; advancing, 20–22; challenges to

faculty, 17–18; connecting, 30; defined,
 24–26; institutional service to support,
 50–51; opportunities to support faculty,
 18–20
Scholarship Assessed, 29
Scholarship of teaching and learning
 (SoTL), 40
*Scholarship Reconsidered: Priorities of the
 Professoriate,* 27, 44
Scholars of Dissemination, 63, 100
Scholars of Pedagogical Practice, 100
Science, technology, engineering, and
 mathematics (STEM), 38
Striving institutions, 57

T

Teaching, scholarship of, 40–42
Temple College (TC), 98
*The Scholarship of Teaching and Learning in
 Higher Education: Contributions of
 Research Universities,* 41
To Improve the Academy, 19

U

Undergraduate research (UR), 49
University of Phoenix, 36
U.S. NewsWorld Report, 74

About the Authors

Vicki L. Baker, PhD, is a professor of economics and management at Albion College in Albion, Michigan. Her research focuses on the role of developmental relationships, at the student and faculty levels, on personal and professional identity development. She also explores institutional change and evolution and the faculty experience in liberal arts colleges. Vicki was the principal investigator of a study of faculty development in a consortium of 13 liberal arts colleges, the Great Lakes Colleges Association (*Initiative for Faculty Development at Liberal Arts Colleges*). That work is featured in the book, *Developing Faculty in Liberal Arts Colleges: Aligning Individual Needs and Organizational Goals* published by Rutgers University Press (with L. G. Lunsford, and M. J. Pifer). She is currently the principal investigator (with L. G. Lunsford, and M. J. Pifer) of a midcareer faculty Academic Leadership Institute (ALI) for the GLCA, funded by the Henry Luce Foundation. Her recent work has appeared in the *Review of Higher Education*, *Journal of Faculty Development*, *Journal of Higher Education*, *To Improve the Academy*, and *Mentoring & Tutoring*. Vicki earned a BS in safety engineering from Indiana University of Pennsylvania, an MBA from Clarion University of Pennsylvania, and MS (management and organizations) and PhD (higher education) degrees from The Pennsylvania State University. She is the co-founder of Lead Mentor Develop, LLC (www.leadmentordevelop.com).

Aimee LaPointe Terosky, EdD, is an associate professor of educational leadership at Saint Joseph's University in Philadelphia, PA. Her research focuses on higher education and K–12 settings with a concentration on teaching, learning, career management, faculty development, instructional leadership, and educational or professional experiences of girls/women. Aimee received her BS in secondary education (social studies) from The Pennsylvania State University, her MA in school leadership from Villanova University, and her EdD in higher and postsecondary education from Teachers College, Columbia University. Aimee received the 2005 Bobby Wright Dissertation of the Year from the Association for the Study of Higher Education. Her work has been published in the *Review of Higher Education, Teachers College Record, Journal of Higher Education, Innovative Higher Education, Journal of Diversity in Higher Education, Studies in Higher Education, Online Learning, Journal of Excellence in College Teaching, Education Administration Quarterly, Journal of School Leadership, School Leadership and Management,* and *Inside Higher Ed.* Additionally, Aimee is the coauthor with KerryAnn O'Meara and Anna Neumann of a 2008 ASHE monograph titled *Faculty Careers and Work Lives: A Professional Growth Perspective.*

Edna Martinez, PhD, is an assistant professor of educational leadership at California State University, San Bernardino in San Bernardino, CA. Her research focuses on issues of access and equity for historically underrepresented students and how organizational behaviors and structures shape their educational experiences and opportunities. Given the overrepresentation of low-income, first-generation students of color in community colleges and Minority Serving Institutions, her work is primarily situated within these contexts. Furthermore, in light of the difference faculty make in outcomes such as student persistence and graduation rates an additional focus she has developed in her research is the study of faculty work and careers. Collectively, her agenda seeks to challenge educational inequities and advance equitable higher education policies and practices. Her work has been published in the *Community College Review, Journal for the Study of Sports and Athletes in Education, Journal of Critical Thought and Praxis, Studies in Higher Education,* and the *International Journal of Doctoral Studies.* She is also the associate editor of the *ASHE Reader Series, Sports and Athletics in Higher Education.* Edna received her BS in biological sciences and her MEd in educational administration from The University of Texas at El Paso and her PhD from Clemson University.

About the ASHE Higher Education Report Series

Since 1983, the ASHE (formerly ASHE-ERIC) Higher Education Report Series has been providing researchers, scholars, and practitioners with timely and substantive information on the critical issues facing higher education. Each monograph presents a definitive analysis of a higher education problem or issue, based on a thorough synthesis of significant literature and institutional experiences. Topics range from planning to diversity and multiculturalism, to performance indicators, to curricular innovations. The mission of the Series is to link the best of higher education research and practice to inform decision making and policy. The reports connect conventional wisdom with research and are designed to help busy individuals keep up with the higher education literature. Authors are scholars and practitioners in the academic community. Each report includes an executive summary, review of the pertinent literature, descriptions of effective educational practices, and a summary of key issues to keep in mind to improve educational policies and practice.

This series is one of the most peer reviewed in higher education. A National Advisory Board made up of ASHE members reviews proposals. A National Review Board of ASHE scholars and practitioners reviews completed manuscripts. Six monographs are published each year, and they are approximately 144 pages in length. The reports are widely disseminated through Jossey-Bass and John Wiley & Sons, and they are available online to subscribing institutions through Wiley Online Library (http://wileyonlinelibrary.com).

Call for Proposals

The ASHE Higher Education Report Series is actively looking for proposals. We encourage you to contact one of the editors, Dr. Kelly Ward (kaward@wsu.edu) or Dr. Lisa Wolf-Wendel (lwolf@ku.edu), with your ideas.

Faculty Members' Scholarly Learning Across Institutional Types

ASHE HIGHER EDUCATION REPORT

ORDER FORM SUBSCRIPTION AND SINGLE ISSUES

DISCOUNTED BACK ISSUES:

Use this form to receive 20% off all back issues of *ASHE Higher Education Report*.
All single issues priced at **$23.20** (normally $29.00)

TITLE   ISSUE NO.   ISBN

_____   _____   _____
_____   _____   _____
_____   _____   _____

Call 1-800-835-6770 or see mailing instructions below. When calling, mention the promotional code JBNND to receive your discount. For a complete list of issues, please visit www.wiley.com/WileyCDA/WileyTitle/productCd-AEHE.html

SUBSCRIPTIONS: (1 YEAR, 6 ISSUES)

☐ New Order   ☐ Renewal

U.S.   ☐ Individual: $174   ☐ Institutional: $347
CANADA/MEXICO   ☐ Individual: $174   ☐ Institutional: $437
ALL OTHERS   ☐ Individual: $210   ☐ Institutional: $491

Call 1-800-835-6770 or see mailing and pricing instructions below.
Online subscriptions are available at www.onlinelibrary.wiley.com

ORDER TOTALS:

Issue / Subscription Amount: $ _____

Shipping Amount: $ _____
(for single issues only – subscription prices include shipping)
Total Amount: $ _____

SHIPPING CHARGES:

First Item $6.00
Each Add'l Item $2.00

(No sales tax for U.S. subscriptions. Canadian residents, add GST for subscription orders. Individual rate subscriptions must be paid by personal check or credit card. Individual rate subscriptions may not be resold as library copies.)

BILLING & SHIPPING INFORMATION:

☐ **PAYMENT ENCLOSED:** *(U.S. check or money order only. All payments must be in U.S. dollars.)*

☐ **CREDIT CARD:**   ☐ VISA   ☐ MC   ☐ AMEX

Card number _____Exp. Date_____

Card Holder Name_____Card Issue # _____

Signature _____Day Phone _____

☐ **BILL ME:** *(U.S. institutional orders only. Purchase order required.)*

Purchase order # _____
Federal Tax ID 13559302 • GST 89102-8052

Name_____
Address_____
Phone_____ E-mail_____

Copy or detach page and send to: **John Wiley & Sons, Inc. / Jossey Bass**
PO Box 55381
Boston, MA 02205-9850

PROMO JBNND